string®

bath shannon **bedfordshire** pink apple designs ltd. **bournemouth** so furniture **bradford** the home **bristol** oskar furniture **cardiff** momentum **cornwall** iroka **dublin** inreda, lost weekend **east yorkshire** ivor innes ltd.
edinburgh the brotique **epping** geoffrey drayton **glasgow** tojo design **henley on thames** central home **kent** papillon interiors **leeds** funktionalley **liverpool** utility **london** future and found ltd, haus, do south, indish,
places and spaces, scp, skandium, twentytwentyone, viaduct **manchester** urbansuite **milton keynes** panik-design **north yorkshire** cimmermann **norwich** design house norwich **nottingham** atomic interiors ltd
oxford central **sheffield** nest.co.uk **suffolk** tea and kate **windsor** urbansuite **selected john lewis stores and johnlewis.com agent** www.pira.info

Miele. Ovens Accurate To Within One Degree.

Miele Artline, our first designer range of built-in appliances for completely flush installation. Pure linear designs epitomise modern living and today's lifestyle, capturing the imagination of architects and interior designers alike. Our expert team of Miele product designers have brought this vision to life with Miele Artline. Gentle opening, handless design, enabled by Miele's innovative Touch2Open and SoftOpen technology.

Precision. Passion. Perfection.

matki | SHOWERING

Matki EauZone Plus

The epitome of luxury, beautifully engineered in the UK

chiara boselli | davide lovatti

MERIDIANI

ELLE
DECORATION
CONTENTS

STYLE

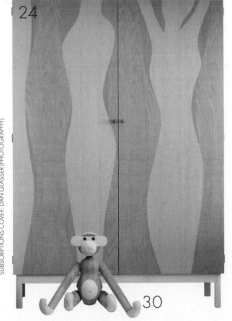

24

30

74

GLOBAL DESIGN

70

COVER

NEWSSTAND
To see more of this month's cover home in Sorrento, decorated with tables by Knoll and Fritz Hansen, as well as Fontana Arte's 'Egg' lamp, turn to p126

SUBSCRIBERS
Our most loyal readers get a closer look at Villa G in France by Studio KO. Discover more stunning projects featured in book *Studio KO* (£55, Rizzoli) on p64

126

ELLE
DECORATION
CONTENTS

HOMES

ESCAPE

**ELLE
DECORATION
BEST OF
BRITISH**

FINALLY

160

Montblanc
5043

Effortless luxury
for modern living

Caesarstone surfaces are a beautiful combination of form and function,
matching high strength, stain resistant engineered quartz with the refined
shades and subtle details of natural stone or hand cast concrete.

Designed and manufactured by the original quartz brand applying
30 years of expertise.

 **caesarstone**®

ELLE
DECORATION

GLOBAL

I'm a proud Brit. Proud of this country and the openness and inclusivity that it represents for me. Not to mention the determination and boundless creativity shown by all those based on this dot of an island, no matter where they may have originated. That said, I also realise that our strength stems from powerful alliances and partnerships, and relies on us playing a crucial role on a global stage.

I've not long returned from the annual Salone del Mobile in Milan, where the world's best new designs are presented during a week of exhibitions, showcases and events. British talent was very much in evidence, but everything I saw really brought home to me the fact that, in the future, isolating ourselves can only be a bad thing, guaranteed to stifle genius, originality and vision.

While in Italy, I also had the pleasure of connecting with many of my fellow editors from the 24 other global editions of ELLE Decoration, sharing ideas and insights, celebrating and cementing our position as the world's biggest interiors magazine brand – collectively, we sell more than two million issues a year! We also handed out our coveted annual awards to the industry's most innovative products and designers.

I returned home determined to put together an issue that would be focused on international greatness, while still championing all things British. Quite a big challenge, but hopefully you'll appreciate our Global Design special, including coverage of our worthy award winners, alongside the absolute best in international architecture, the hottest hotel interiors and cutting-edge design boutiques around the world.

Plus, as our minds turn to the prospect of holiday escapes in sunnier climes, I was also keen that *all* of this month's exceptional homes would be available to rent, so that, in theory, any of us could live the ELLE Decoration dream – even if just for a week or two this summer.

Ben Spriggs

Executive Editor

PICTURE: JAMES MCNAUGHT

Follow me on ⬛ Instagram: @mrbspriggs 🐦 Twitter: @ELLEDecoBen ➕ Visit elledecoration.co.uk

ELLE DECORATION

House of Hearst, 30 Panton Street, London SW1Y 4AJ
Editorial enquiries elledecoration@hearst.co.uk (020 7434 1044)
Homes submissions homes@elledecoration.co.uk

GROUP EDITORIAL DIRECTOR
SUSY SMITH

PA to Group Editorial Director Sandra Tear

EXECUTIVE EDITOR
BEN SPRIGGS

GROUP EDITORIAL PRODUCTION
Workflow Director Carly Levy
Group Managing Editor Ingrid Eames
Chief Sub-Editors Clare Sartin,
Michele Jameson, Helen Bonthrone
Deputy Chief Sub-Editor Julie Pannell-Rae
Sub-Editor Rebecca Hastings

ART
Art Director Philippe Blanchin
Art Editors Roger Browning, Kirstie Bird
Junior Designers Jack Melrose, Victoria Smith

PICTURES
Picture Director Patricia Taylor
Picture Editor Anita Isaacs
Picture Researcher Phoebe Lowndes

FEATURES
Features Editor Amy Moorea Wong
Senior Features Writer Charlotte Brook

HOMES
Content Director Pip McCormac
Interiors Editor Kiera Buckley-Jones

Contributors Amy Bradford, Eliza Honey, Emma Love, Becky Sunshine, Sarah Slade,
Hannah Bort, Sania Pell, Amanda Smith-Corston, Suzanne Stankus, James Williams

**CHIEF BRAND OFFICER,
LIFESTYLE & HOMES**
SHARON DOUGLAS
PA to Chief Brand Officer
Helen Hart
**Brand Development Director,
Lifestyle & Homes**
Alistair Wood

CLIENT DIVISION
Managing Director, Beauty
Jacqui Cave
Managing Director, Fashion & Luxury
Jacqueline Euwe
Managing Director, Fitness & Health
Alun Williams
Director of Endorsements & Food
Laura Cohen
Director of Travel
Denise Degroot
Director of Motors
Jim Chaudry
Client Director, Personal Finance
Jacquie Duckworth

AGENCY DIVISION
Chief Agency Officer
Jane Wolfson
Executive Assistant
Tanya Stewart 020 7439 5532
Lifestyle Group Regional Director
Lisa Bhatti 016 1962 9254
Lifestyle Group Agency Director
Matthew Downs 020 7339 4583

ENQUIRIES
Senior Client Manager
Stephanie Tomlinson 020 7439 5462
Client Executive
Maire Power 020 7439 5650
Head of Business Management
Lucy Porter 020 7439 5276
Business Manager Rose Sweetman
Head of Classified Lee Rimmer 020 3728 7707

BRAND LICENSING
Managing Director, Business Services
Judith Secombe

CONSUMER SALES & MARKETING
Marketing & Circulation Director
Reid Holland
Head of Consumer Sales & Marketing
James Hill
Head of Marketing Promotions
Aoibheann Foley
Head of Subscriptions
Karen Sharp
Digital Marketing Director
Seema Kumari

COMMUNICATIONS
Interim Head of PR & Communications
Debra Johnson
PR Manager
Alice Taylor
Journalist Enquiries
media@hearst.co.uk

PRODUCTION
Production Manager Stephen Osbourne
Ad Production Coordinator Carl Latter

HEARST UK
President & CEO
James Wildman
Chief Finance Officer/Chief Operating Officer
Claire Blunt
Director of Events & Sponsorship, Hearst Live
Victoria Archbold
Chief Operations Director
Clare Gorman
Chief Strategy Officer
Robert Ffitch
HR Director
Surinder Simmons

HEARST MAGAZINES INTERNATIONAL
**Senior Vice President/CFO
& General Manager**
Simon Horne
**Senior Vice President/Editorial
& Brand Director**
Kim St Clair Bodden

LAGARDÈRE ACTIVE
Chairman and CEO Lagardère Active
Denis Olivennes
CEO ELLE France & International
Constance Benqué
CEO ELLE International Media Licenses
François Coruzzi
Brand Management of ELLE Decoration
Sylvie de Chirée
SVP/International Director of ELLE Decoration
Valéria Bessolo Llopiz
**SVP/Director of International
Media Licenses, Digital Development
& Syndication** Mickaël Berret
Editorial Executive of ELLE Decoration
Linda Bergmark
Marketing Executive of ELLE Decoration
Morgane Rohee
Syndication Coordinator Audrey Schneuwly

INTERNATIONAL AD SALES HOUSE
Lagardère Global Advertising CEO
François Coruzzi
SVP/International Advertising
Stéphanie Delattre
stephanie.delattre@lagardere-active.com
Lagardère Global Advertising, 10 rue Thierry
Le Luron 92300 Levallois- Per ret, France

BACK ISSUES & SUBSCRIPTIONS
Hearst Magazines UK, Tower House, Sovereign Park,
Market Harborough, Leicestershire LE16 9EF
To order or renew a subscription, telephone
01858 438846 or fax 01858 461739
For any other subscription enquiries, telephone 01858
438880 or email elledecoration@subscription.co.uk.
Lines open Mon–Fri 8am–9pm; Sat 8am–4pm.
Standard rates for 12 issues: UK £52.80; Eire & Europe
Airmail £55; USA £65; Rest Of The World £75

PRINTED BY Wyndeham Roche Ltd, St Austell
COVER PRINTED BY Westdale, Cardiff
PAPER SUPPLIED BY Burgo Group
DISTRIBUTION BY Frontline Ltd, Peterborough
Tel 01733 555161

TRADEMARK NOTICE
ELLE® and ELLE Decoration™ are used under licence
from the trademark owner, Hachette Filipacchi Presse
ELLE Decoration is a member of the Independent
Press Standards Organisation and abides by the
Editors' Code of Practice. We are committed to
upholding the highest standards of journalism. If you
think that we have not met those standards and want
to make a complaint, contact complaints@hearst.co.uk
or visit hearst.co.uk/hearst-magazines-uk-
complaints-procedure. If we are unable to resolve
your complaint, or if you would like more information
about IPSO or the Editors' Code, contact IPSO on
0300 123 2220 or visit ipso.co.uk

**AUGUST ISSUE ON SALE
5 JULY 2018**

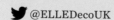 

FLEXFORM

FLEXFORM | **MADE IN ITALY**

Home at last.

SUBSCRIBE TO ELLE DECORATION
SAVE 30%*

Every issue of ELLE Decoration is packed full of inspiration, information and ideas, with a mix of styles, products and price points that will help you make your home stylish

GREAT REASONS TO SUBSCRIBE

■ *JUST £39.99 for your first 12 issues**

■ Receive **LIMITED EDITION** subscriber-only covers

■ *FREE delivery direct to your door every month*

■ *Join the* **ELLE DECORATION VIP CLUB** *and enjoy exclusive offers*

~~£57.60~~
YOU PAY
£39.99*

DESIGN PORTRAIT.

Ray, seat system designed by Antonio Citterio. www.bebitalia.com

B&B Italia Store London, SW3 2AS - 250 Brompton Road - T. +44 020 7591 8111 - info.bromptonroad@bebitalia.com
UK Agent: Ben Ritson - T. +44 793 1556345 - sales@ritsondesign.com

B&B
ITALIA

ELLE
DECORATION
STYLE

DESIGN / **PEOPLE** / **DECORATING** / **ARCHITECTURE**   *Edited by* **BECKY SUNSHINE**

GIVE ME *SHELTER*

Kettal's 'PH1' pavilions can be put together in different combinations to suit your garden's needs – ceiling panels include waterproof and slatted options, while side panels can incorporate blinds, curtains, shelving or glass. From £14,915 (kettal.com).

CATCHPOLE & RYE

KENT ENGLAND

CATCHPOLE & RYE
KENT ENGLAND

SITTING *PRETTY*

Japanese furniture brand Maruni, which celebrates its 90th anniversary this year, has worked with longtime collaborator Jasper Morrison to create the 'Fugu' chair. 'The idea was to create a wooden seat so comfortable it wouldn't need upholstery,' says Morrison of his elegant, lightly curved design made from solid oak. From £1,500 (maruni.com).

PICTURE: CHRIS TONNESEN

IN THE **ROUND**

The gentle curves of Danish design brand Space Copenhagen's new 'Gleda' lounge table for Benchmark will lend minimalist homes a soft, organic feel. The table comes in two height options, and a choice of sustainable natural, whitened, aged or ebonised oak. From £795 (benchmarkfurniture.com).

SHAPED BY THE CLASSICS

Using steam-bending techniques, Benjamin Hubert of design studio Layer has created a smooth, curved timber basket for Fritz Hansen. Inspired by the mid-century furniture that the iconic Danish brand is known for, the piece is available in natural oak, stained oak and walnut. From £209 (fritzhansen.com).

3 OF THE BEST
CONTEMPORARY RATTAN

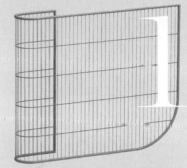

'NASSA' SCREEN BY MARTA AYALA HERRERA FOR YAMAKAWA RATTAN

Spanish designer Herrera's fresh style teamed with this brand's know-how has resulted in an ultra-modern piece. From £1,769 (yamakawa-rattan.com).

'PAL' STOOL BY SAMI KALLIO FOR NORTHERN

The rattan top on this three-legged seat by Finnish-born, Gothenburg-based designer Kallio lends it extra charm. From £237.49, Clippings (clippings.com).

'THE RATTAN VENUS CHAIR' BY SOANE BRITAIN

This delicately scalloped seat with a forged metal base is handmade in the brand's specialist rattan workshop in Leicestershire. £5,900 (soane.co.uk).

IN FULL *BLOOM*

The meadow of pink carnations at designer Tory Burch's AW18 catwalk show (below) signalled a flurry of florals coming our way this summer. Here, we look at three ways to bring the trend home

PAPER VASE COVERS BY PEPE HEYKOOP

To produce these sleeves, which add colour to plain vases, Heykoop works with the Tiny Miracles Foundation, paying women of Mumbai's Pardeshi community to make them. Profits go towards education and healthcare. £18, Aram (aram.co.uk).

'CLEF DES CHAMPS' WALLCOVERING BY FROMENTAL

Proudly display your love of flowers by turning a wall into a meadow, with this exquisite hand-painted and embroidered design. Price on request (fromental.co.uk).

HOMEWARE BY LA DOUBLEJ

This Italian brand's 'Housewives' tableware by Ancap (£65 for a plate) serves up an elaborate take on florals. More petals adorn its glass *tipetti* (ornamental goblets; £3,500 each), made by Murano-based glassware company Salviati (ladoublej.com).

Called the Society Table, the design unites premium wood, leather, glass and steel in a simple, expressive form with a timeless aesthetic.

CARL HANSEN & SØN
PASSIONATE CRAFTSMANSHIP

NATURAL *DELICACY*

Add a faint blush of copper and pink to gracefully curved accessories, Scandi-style wooden furniture and woven textures

1 'Elan' **armoire**, £8,450, Pinch (pinchdesign.com) **2** 'Zip' **wallpaper** by Christian Benini, £286 per roll, Wall & Decò (wallanddeco.com) **3** 'Semi' **pendant light** in copper by Claus Bonderup and Torsten Thorup for Gubi, from £549, The Conran Shop (conranshop.co.uk) **4** 'Dojo' **table** by Amandine Chhor and Aïssa Logerot for Petite Friture, £1,865, Clippings (clippings.com) **5** 'Handle' **vase** by Eva Harlou, £75, Mater (materdesign.com) **6** Breakfast **bowl** by Leu Ceramics, £32, The London Smiths (thelondonsmiths.com) **7** 'Noli' **chair** by Ludovica and Roberto Palomba for Zanotta, from £600, Chaplins (chaplins.co.uk) **8** 'Garden Layers' **rug** in 'Diagonal Almond Ivory' by Gandia Blasco, £799, Heal's (heals.com)

COMPILED BY: KIERA BUCKLEY-JONES PICTURE: MIRO ZAGNOLI

OUTSIDE INFLUENCERS

Designed to weather summer storms – but with style credentials worthy of any interior – these new seats are the perfect update for your garden

'TRIANGLE' CHAIR, STELLAR WORKS

Adapted from its original wooden version, created in 1952 for Denmark's Louisiana Museum of Modern Art, designer Vilhelm Wohlert's chair has been reissued in outdoor-ready aluminium. £816 (stellarworks.com).

'BREA' SOFA, DEDON

The star of UK design duo Barber & Osgerby's second collection for German outdoor furniture brand Dedon is this modular sofa, built around a simple tubular frame. It has slip-on covers that can be removed speedily at the first sign of wet weather. Available January 2019 (dedon.de).

THE BEST NEW *DESIGN BOOKS*

We reveal the two tomes that will be gracing the most stylish coffee tables this summer

Libby Sellers

Women Design

—

Pioneers in architecture, industrial, graphic and digital design from the twentieth century to the present day

WOMEN DESIGN BY LIBBY SELLERS

Design historian, author, gallerist and former curator at London's Design Museum Libby Sellers' new book profiles the lives and work of 21 of the world's most prominent female creatives. Pioneers such as Eileen Gray, Ray Eames and Eva Zeisel are celebrated alongside today's innovators, from Neri Oxman to Patricia Urquiola and Nathalie du Pasquier. It's a fascinating insight into the women who have shaped the way we live (£20, Francis Lincoln).

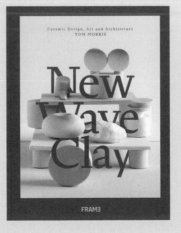

NEW WAVE CLAY: CERAMIC DESIGN, ART AND ARCHITECTURE BY TOM MORRIS

Design journalist Morris has seized upon the current appetite for all things craft with his latest book. Delving into the world of experimental ceramic furniture, murals, vessels, 3D printing and even clay-based buildings, he shines a light on 55 exciting designers at the very forefront of the movement (£32, Frame).

SUMMER *ESSENTIAL*

The brand new volume of ELLE Decoration Country is out now. It's your invite to the world's most beautiful homes in the countryside, packed with seasonal style inspiration, breathtaking views and our edit of the pieces that will help you recreate the pared-back look in your own home. And all for just £9.99. Order online (with free post and packaging) at hearstmagazines.co.uk/elle-decoration-specials or pick up your copy at selected WHSmith stores.

STYLE YOUR HOME LIKE THE NED

Soho Home has released a brand new collection based on the old-world luxury of its newest London hotel – already the capital's hottest venue

When designer Adam Greco, along with his colleagues Alice Lund and Rebecca King, began work on the interior of The Ned (located in the Sir Edwin Lutyens-designed former Midland Bank) over four years ago, owner Nick Jones' brief was for faded glamour.

'We designed The Ned to feel not only like a grand hotel, but to also have the comfort of an old country house,' says Greco. 'It's unabashedly ornate, taking on traditional, formal styles in a louche way.'

> 'We designed The Ned to feel not only like a grand hotel, but to have the comfort of an old country house'

Fans of the hotel can achieve its luxurious look at home with Soho Home's accompanying collection. Highlights include stylish iron-framed beds and headboards upholstered in William Morris fabrics (inspired by the look of the first-class cabins on the Titanic), velvet sofas with pleated backs and Art Deco-style mirrors. Every detail is considered, from the bankers' green used for the reworked archive pattern on the 'Burleigh' china to the pick of sumptuous dusty pink, teal and burnt orange shades for the cushions (sohohome.com).

PICTURE: SIMON BROWN

'Cosy' bed in bronze, £1,695; headboard upholstered in 'Artichoke' fabric by William Morris, from £595; 'Monroe' cushion in 'Burnt Orange', £50, all Soho Home

'Lutyens' opal glass and antique brass pendant light, £495

'Banner' round velvet cushion in 'Dusky Pink', £60

'Burleigh Hibiscus' cereal bowl, £20

'Margot' buttoned linen footstool, £545

'Edwin' velvet three-seater sofa in 'Dusky Pink', £3,995

INSIDE STORY BRDR KRÜGER

This 132-year-old Danish brand's minimalist style and attention to detail have kept it at the forefront of design

The 'ARV' round table (£2,831) and chairs (£1,239 each) by Studio David Thulstrup in Noma 2.0

Pure in form but playful in spirit, each Brdr Krüger piece has a tactile charm, thanks to the way the wood is refined by hand until silky smooth

'Bølling' tray table by Hans Bølling, £449

'Monkey' by Kay Bojesen for Rosendahl, from £108

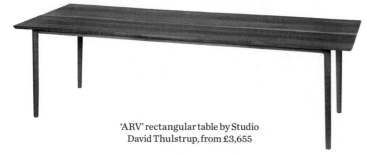

'ARV' rectangular table by Studio David Thulstrup, from £3,655

For Jonas and Jyliane Krüger – the fifth generation of Copenhagen-based brand Brdr Krüger, founded in 1886 – working with Danish architect David Thulstrup on the new 'ARV' furniture collection (above) for chef René Redzepi's Noma 2.0 restaurant in the Danish capital was a dream come true. 'We value the same honesty and integrity in materials that Thulstrup does, as well as the beauty of craftsmanship,' says Jonas, the company's creative director.

Brdr Krüger's ability as a small family business (Brdr stands for brothers, in honour of the company's founding siblings, Theodor and Ferdinand) to respond and innovate quickly was what attracted Thulstrup to work with the brand. From first sketch to final production, the process of designing and manufacturing Thulstrup's 'ARV' range took just three months. Using traditional joinery techniques and precision engineering, the brand creates modern pieces with a distinct lack of ornamentation. Traditional wooden dowels and discreet magnets replace nails and screws, and attention is given to fine hand-finishing.

Since its early wood-turning days, making lamps for churches and Copenhagen's famous Tivoli Gardens, Brdr Krüger has produced many recognisable pieces, including Danish architect Hans Bølling's iconic 'Bølling' tray table (a staple of many Scandinavian homes) and Kay Bojesen's wooden monkey for Rosendahl – more than 1,000 monkeys, in four different sizes, are made every week. There's also the brand's ever-growing collection of furniture, created in collaboration with rising stars of the design world, such as Thomas Lykke (who also designed the company's stylish new showroom), Rasmus Bækkel Fex and Sverre Uhnger.

Pure in form but playful in spirit, each Brdr Krüger piece has a tactile charm, thanks to the way the wood is refined by hand until silky smooth. 'To have the right quality, you need experienced craftspeople,' says Jonas. 'We're building on the past to step into the future.' *brdr-kruger.com*

kirkby**design**

contemporary textiles for interiors

kirkby**design**.com

HISTORY OF A BRAND LOUIS POULSEN

An illuminating look at the legendary Danish lighting company that boasts creations by some of the most iconic architects and designers of our time

Though its history dates back to 1874, when it was founded as a wine importer by Ludvig R Poulsen, one could argue that Louis Poulsen's true story as one of the world's most influential lighting companies began in 1924. That year, an amateur Danish architect named Poul Henningsen (below) approached Louis Poulsen & Co – by then known as a purveyor of electrical goods – with an idea for a light he wanted to present at the Paris Exposition Internationale des Arts Decoratifs et Industriels Modernes. The design came with a set of three shades, which concealed the lightbulb and gave off direct and indirect light that was warm and flattering. The concept won the Paris Exposition 1925 gold medal, and the very next year, together with Louis Poulsen, Henningsen was tasked with lighting the Forum Building in Copenhagen, where the first 'PH' pendant lights were debuted to much critical success. That same year, Louis Poulsen published its first lighting catalogue.

By 1958, Henningsen had produced two more breakthrough designs: the 72-leaved 'PH Artichoke' pendant for Copenhagen's Langelinie Pavillonen restaurant and the 'PH 5', which included an additional shade for uplighting. Both Henningsen and Louis Poulsen had become household names,

so much so that when architect Arne Jacobsen was tasked with designing the SAS Royal Hotel in Copenhagen in 1960, he turned to the company to manufacture his designs for the 'AJ' table (above), wall and floor lamps and the 'AJ Royal' pendant, all intrinsic parts of his *'Gesamtwerk'* (total work) philosophy, which saw him design not only the hotel, but every detail of its interiors. The list of illustrious names Louis Poulsen has worked with since is a who's-who of the world's design scene: Verner Panton, Foster + Partners, GamFratesi, Clara Von Zweigbergk, Oki Sato of Nendo and many, many more.

In 2011, Louis Poulsen became the first lighting manufacturer to win the American Institute of Architects award for 'Collaborative Achievement' – and for good reason. The brand constantly updates its designs: whether it's making the 'AJ' wall lights using LEDs for outdoor use, or releasing six new, cheerful colours for the 'PH 5' on its 60th anniversary this year. And this doesn't just apply to the classics: Swedish designer Clara Von Zweigbergk's bright 'Cirque' pendant lights from 2016 were recently re-released in a palette of greys. Perhaps Henningsen's greatest legacy to Louis Poulsen was the never-ending quest for lighting perfection. *louispoulsen.com*

WORDS: ELIZA HONEY PICTURE: WETOUCH IMAGEWORK

THE EDIT
FIVE DESIGNS TO KNOW

'PH Artichoke' pendant light designed by Poul Henningsen in 1958, £6,200

'Cirque' pendant light by Clara Von Zweigbergk, updated in a new grey palette, £220

'Doo-Wop' pendant light, developed in the 1950s, from £310

'Panthella Mini' table lamp, an updated version of Verner Panton's 1971 design, £470

'PH 5 Mini' pendant light by Poul Henningsen in fresh colours, £444

DESIGN HERO
WARD BENNETT

The understated designer whose simple, minimalist style was influenced by religion, nature and art

New York-born Ward Bennett (1917–2003) was celebrated in his lifetime for the elegant simplicity of his furniture, tableware, textiles and interiors. He is associated with the early minimalism of the 1970s, popular then only with the ultra-hip. Yet the roots of his pared-down, monastic aesthetic were complex – founded on an admiration for medieval Cistercian abbeys and the work of philosopher Henry David Thoreau, who ignited his passion for Zen Buddhism.

Bennett drove inexpensive cars and, like a Beat poet, dressed mainly in black clothing. Paradoxically, while he created more than 100 chairs – motivated partly by bad back pain – he preferred built-in seating. 'It's the space that's important. Although I design furniture, I also love to eliminate it,' said Bennett, who is considered a pioneer of the conversation pit (sunken seating).

Born Howard Bernstein – his father was vaudeville actor Murray Bennett – he left home aged 13 because of family clashes and taught himself the principles of design, his thirst for culture and travel making up for his lack of formal training. In the 1930s, after working as a shipping clerk, he took off to Europe and, in Paris,

'It's the space that's important. Although I design furniture, I also love to eliminate it'

studied under artist Constantin Brâncuşi, whose sculptures he admired enormously. On Bennett's return to New York City, fashion house Hattie Carnegie hired him as a designer and window-dresser. In the 1940s, he was briefly a sculptor, and also learned to make jewellery in Mexico.

In 1947, Bennett created one of the first of the understated interiors that would typify his style – a Manhattan penthouse with white lacquered bookshelves and cork floors. Long before the 1970s high-tech trend took hold, he repurposed industrial elements for domestic use. For his holiday house in East Hampton, he used a manhole guard rail as a modern towel rack, while the entrance to his minimal, monochrome apartment on Manhattan's Upper West Side was via a sleek galley kitchen.

His furniture, originally created for Brickel Associates, includes the industrial-looking 'I Beam' table, 'Scissor' chair (right) and 'Envelope' side chair (left), with a leather seat stretched over a slimline frame (all available from Herman Miller), and he also designed glassware and cutlery for Tiffany & Co. Yet, despite its influence, Bennett's work has never been well documented – until now, that is. Elizabeth Beer and Brian Janusiak's *Ward Bennett* monograph finally gives the designer the attention he so rightly deserves.

Clockwise from top Ward Bennett with a collection of 'Shellback' sofas and chairs. The 'Scissor' chair by Ward Bennett for Herman Miller. The 'Envelope' chair, designed in 1966 for Herman Miller and in production ever since

Left New book *Ward Bennett* by Elizabeth Beer and Brian Janusiak (£59.95, Phaidon)

WORDS: DOMINIC LUTYENS. PICTURES: MICHAEL PATEMAN/HERMAN MILLER ARCHIVES

MY CULTURAL LIFE
BELLA FREUD

A style icon on what they're reading, watching, listening to and more

London-born Bella Freud launched her eponymous fashion label in 1990, and has since brought her bookish brand of cool to collaborations with heritage British labels from Biba to Barbour. Now, she is turning to interiors: Freud recently transposed the slogans that adorn her cult jumpers – song lyrics, catchphrases and the perky-eared whippet drawn by her father, the painter Lucien Freud – onto cushions, blankets and candles. This year, alongside Retrouvius' Maria Speake (who worked on Freud's home and her brand's London store, **1**), she has designed a penthouse in the Grade II-listed BBC Television Centre in White City. 'It feels natural and exciting,' Freud says of working on the apartment, which opens and goes on sale to the public in September (@bella_freud; bellafreud.com; televisioncentre.com).

My all-time favourite piece of music is probably Nick Cave's *No More Shall We Part*. It is exquisite, so sad and so uplifting. Bob Marley's *Get Up Stand Up* also springs to mind. When I first heard it at 13, it was like an inspiring call to arms.

I'm now listening to Richard Russell's *Everything is Recorded* – the album has a lot of minor chords, which I love, but have to watch out for if I'm feeling melancholy.

A track that makes me feel instantly happy is *Walk This Way* by Run DMC, which I often play in the morning. It peps me up and reminds me of my best self.

The book that has influenced me the most is Jack Kerouac's *The Dharma Bums*. When I read it, aged 14, it was like an electric shock. I was entranced by the rhythm of his words. Reading Malcolm X's autobiography

(**3**) had a very profound effect on me, too. It made me excruciatingly aware of racism and my self-righteous prejudices in a way that I hadn't previously appreciated.

I've been reading *The Andy Warhol Diaries* for ages, which is great for when I'm feeling anxious as it's both bland and interesting. I like to have a few books on the go – I'm finishing Donna Tartt's *A Secret History*, which is the opposite, almost too disturbing, and have just started *Chelsea Girls* by the poet Eileen Myles.

My top five film list goes as follows: *Apocalypse Now*, *Some Like It Hot* (**4**), *The Producers*, *Freaks* and *La Grande Illusion*. They are like part of my DNA. Oh, and I must add Ken Loach's *Kes*. I saw it when I was ten or 11 and was so moved that I have never dared watch it again.

My favourite gallery is the Courtauld Institute (**5**) at Somerset House, where I always look at Manet's *A Bar at the Folies-Bergère*.

The last exhibition I saw was the Picasso 1932 show at Tate Modern, all about his passion for Marie-Thérèse Walter and the amazing portraits he painted of her (**2**). It was horribly crowded, though – everyone obviously wanted to get in on the love.

My formula for a fun night... If I get a chance to dance my head off, preferably with a gay man, then I know I'll be happy.

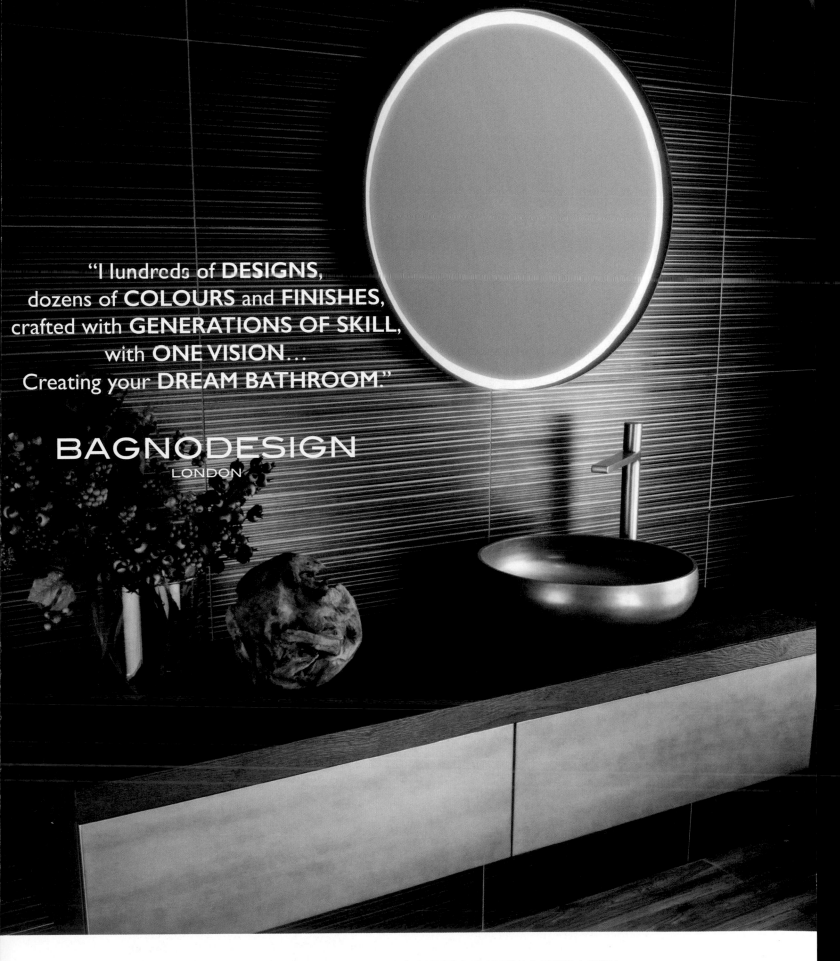

"Hundreds of DESIGNS,
dozens of COLOURS and FINISHES,
crafted with GENERATIONS OF SKILL,
with ONE VISION…
Creating your DREAM BATHROOM."

BAGNODESIGN
LONDON

DECORATING /

SPRING FORWARD

Amusingly named after the tumbling spring toy for children, the 'Slinkie' collection of rugs by Patricia Urquiola for CC-Tapis features three designs. Each is inspired by organic shapes, as well as the colour wheel, with tonal graduations realised in soft Himalayan wool. From £4,769 (cc-tapis.com).

WABI-SABI WALLS

'Shades of Pale', the new collection of wallcoverings by Brian Yates, is influenced by the materials used in traditional Japanese interiors. We're drawn to the undulating texture of this basket-woven raffia. Other designs are made from bamboo, jute and sisal and all come in understated, muted tones, making them the perfect backdrop to a tranquil decorating scheme. Raffia weave on non-woven backing, £185 per metre (brian-yates.co.uk).

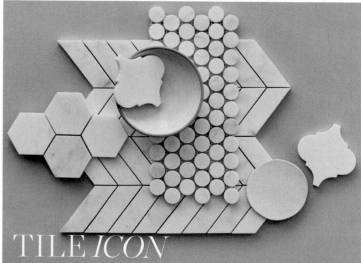

TILE ICON

New tiling brand Claybrook, based in London's Shoreditch, offers 26 styles for walls and floors in a variety of sizes, prints and colours – from the glass geometric 'Confiserie' to the encaustic 'Old Havana' and the classically beautiful marble mosaic 'Brookhaven' (above). Order online or visit to discuss your needs with the in-house design team. From £39 per square metre (claybrookstudio.co.uk).

EURO STAR

Now available in a range of new shapes – including rectangular, lozenge, diamond and circle varieties – Clé's stylish 'Belgian Reproduction' tiles pay homage to designs that can be found on the floors of the grand courtyards of northern Europe. Handcrafted from wood-fired terracotta, they are unglazed and have a delightful aged patina. From £179.50 per square metre (cletile.com).

FLAWLESS *FLOORING*

Ecora, an interiors company known for its sustainable and ecologically responsible products, has added a choice of 40 new finishes to its existing range. We love 'Oak Hoxton' – a smoked oak with dark brown and black tones – in the 'Mansion Weave' pattern. £160 per square metre (ecora.co.uk).

ROCKETT *POWERED*

Jane Rockett and Lucy St George, co-founders of homeware brand Rockett St George, have turned their hands to designing wallpaper. The five new patterns – which include a Gothic lace design and a leopard print – all display a hint of the rock-and-roll aesthetic that the firm is known for. Our favourite is 'Oriental Garden' (below), with bold Chinoiserie motifs. £99 per roll (rockettstgeorge.co.uk).

SHADES OF **SKYE**

When professional decorator Alasdair Campbell couldn't find an exterior paint that would withstand the dramatic weather of the Isle of Skye, he took matters into his own hands and set up the Isle of Skye Paint Company. There are 32 colours, all of which reflect the island's landscape, and can be used indoors and out. From £24.50 for 2.5 litres (isleofskye paintcompany.co.uk).

JOIN THE *GUILD*

Designers Guild's flagship store on London's King's Road is now bigger than ever, with a new space dedicated purely to its extensive range of wallpapers, fabrics and paints. It's a true one-stop shop for all your decorating needs (designersguild.com).

WORDS: KIERA BUCKLEY-JONES
PICTURES: LAURIE FRANKEL, SIMON MAXWELL

DESIGN DETAILS EXTERIOR PAINT

While the sun is shining, take the opportunity to refresh your home's façade, fences and more with a lick of the latest durable colours

What should I choose? Masonry paints are suitable for walls, bricks and render, but there are also specialist paints for metals and wood. As with those for interior walls, exterior paints come in different finishes, such as eggshell, satin and gloss, so think about the look you want to achieve. It's also worth remembering that most paints can't be applied in temperatures below 5°C, or if there's a risk of rain or frost – so summer is the best time to refresh outdoor spaces.

How do I tackle mould? Look for products with mould-resistant and weatherproof formulas. A brick waterproofing product, for example, will protect against ice, rain and snow, and can be used in tandem with regular masonry paints. Limewash is also a good option for walls prone to damp.

What other preparation do I need to do? 'Make sure to remove any surface dirt and loose paint with a scraper and a stiff-bristled brush,' says Kasia Wiktorowicz, marketing communications manager at Valspar. 'If the wall is very dirty, wash it with a household detergent and rinse well with water. Ensure any small cracks and holes are filled and sanded down, and then use an exterior primer to prepare the surface for painting.' Applying an undercoat is also a good idea, as it gives the new colour opacity and helps to cover up previous paint jobs.

How often do exterior surfaces need to be repainted? Most outdoor paints have been designed to give between ten and 15 years of protection from the elements.

What colour should I choose? 'If you're painting walls or fences in the garden, the shade you select should add to your outdoor space, rather than detracting from it,' explains David Mottershead. 'Gardens already have their own accent colours provided by the plants you choose, so use these as your starting palette.'

1. BEST FOR ECO-FRIENDLY LIMEWASH

BAUWERK

This Australian company specialises in natural lime paint, which absorbs into the wall and allows the surface to breathe. Suitable for all masonry, but not wooden doors or trims. No undercoat or sealer needed. **Pictured** 'Saint Germain' lime paint, £31 for one litre (bauwerkcolour.co.uk).

2. BEST FOR EGGSHELL

FARROW & BALL

Eggshell paint is perfect for adding a silky sheen to exterior wood and metal surfaces, but Farrow & Ball also has fantastic matt, quick-drying and water-based masonry paints in its 132 colours. **Pictured** 'Cook's Blue' masonry paint, £80 for five litres (farrow-ball.com).

3. BEST FOR MULTIPLE FINISHES

LITTLE GREENE

From quick-drying gloss to exterior eggshell and masonry paints, Little Greene offers a wide range of outdoor solutions. There's also 'Tom's Oil' eggshell, which gives woodwork and metal a traditional finish. **Pictured** 'Yellow-Pink' masonry paint, £65 for five litres (littlegreene.com).

4. BEST FOR COLOUR SELECTION

VALSPAR

Choose from around 200 garden and decking paint shades. Still not able to find the exact hue you want? The brand's colour matching service, available at B&Q, allows you to create bespoke options. **Pictured** 'Peach Parfait' masonry paint, £25 for 2.5 litres (valsparpaint.co.uk).

5. BEST FOR A CHALKY LOOK

DESIGNERS GUILD

Hardwearing and offering protection from the elements, this water-based masonry paint can be used on walls, bricks and render. A low, five per cent sheen level gives it an attractive chalky, matt appearance. **Pictured** 'Pale Jade' masonry paint, £44 for 2.5 litres (designersguild.com).

ARAM STORE SALE

London's Best Modern Furniture Store (Est 1964)

SALE
STARTS 16 JUNE

BIG DISCOUNTS
OFF EX-DISPLAY FURNITURE

15% OFF
ALL NEW ORDERS*

*Not in conjunction with any other discounted price or sale price offer.
Some exclusions apply online.

ARAM STORE 110 DRURY LANE, COVENT GARDEN, LONDON WC2B 5SG | TEL: 020 7557 7557
MONDAY – SATURDAY 10AM – 6PM (THURS UNTIL 7PM) SUNDAYS IN SALE 11AM – 5PM

WWW.ARAM.CO.UK

COLOUR AQUA

*This blue-green hue has a history as vast
as the calm, summery seas it resembles*

**PANTONE®
325 C**

In Homer's *Odyssey*, on his return home, the hero meets Proteus, known also as the Old Man of the Sea. Proteus is one of the stranger deities in the Greek pantheon: he has the gift of prophesy, but hates using it, so to get the truth, you have to hold him down while he squirms and transforms himself into myriad shapes – tigers, snakes, even water itself – trying to break free. Given this attribute, Proteus is the god most associated with the variable nature of oceans, rivers and lakes. The word 'protean', taken from his name, means changeable – and it feels appropriate that water should have a god dedicated to its inconstancy. Even its colour is up for debate. Homer famously referred to it as 'wine-dark'; James Joyce, in his Modernist take on the Greek writer's epic, was less effusive. 'The sea,' he wrote, 'the snotgreen sea'.

Water, as everyone knows, has moods. If the sea is stormy and treacherous one evening, you might well wake the next morning to find it pale blue and becalmed. Navy one moment; brown-grey with beige-tipped waves the next. The reason we tend to think of it as blue is complicated. In a glass, of course, it usually looks clear, but if water is deep enough, more of the longer wavelengths – reds and yellows – are absorbed, leaving the shorter wavelengths to be scattered, thus making calmer, clearer water more likely to appear greenish blue.

Another reason why we tend to immediately associate water with the colour blue is cultural. Perhaps due to advertising, holiday memories or childhood imagery – seas are nearly always perfectly azure in picture books. Aqua's watery associations lend it some ocean-like attributes: it's refreshing, summery, nautical, a little mysterious and very capacious. Aquas come in almost as many shades as the sea itself: near-turquoise, minty, dark teal or the clear, untroubled blue of the aquamarine stone.

In our homes, this colour can be taken in many design directions. One is the more synthetic, mid-century route, with less grey and perhaps a dash more blue. Think icy movie-goddess dresses deepening to that tint redolent of Studebaker cars – this works better on accessories than on whole walls, where its single-mindedness soon palls. The inkier, greyer aqua hues have a more modern feel. Little Greene's 'Turquoise Blue' (see above right) feels clean and refreshing, making it perfect for bathrooms or kitchens. Toe-dippers might try Claire Gaudion's abstract 'Rhythmic Tides' rug (£359; clairegaudion.com), which includes several of the sea's infinite hues, from wine-dark to… let's call it green.

PAINTS TO TRY

'Turquoise Blue', £43.50 for 2.5 litres, Little Greene (littlegreene.com)

'Deep Water Green', £48.50 for 2.5 litres, Paint & Paper Library (paintandpaperlibrary.com)

'Marine', £44 for 2.5 litres, Designers Guild (designersguild.com)

FARROW&BALL

CRAFTSMEN IN PAINT AND PAPER

MORE THAN COLOUR

There's an exact science to combining the finest quality ingredients within our closely guarded formulas.
It's what gives our paint its extraordinary depth and lasting finish.

KITCHENS & BATHROOMS /

FLOATING ON AIR

Designed with open-plan living in mind, the new '+Venovo' kitchen by Poggenpohl – including an island, tall unit and sideboard – looks as though it is suspended mid-air, thanks to its refined metal supports. It's available in the brand's seven signature colours, as well as a wood veneer, with legs in chrome, satin black or white. From £35,000 (poggenpohl.com).

I'M WITH THE BAND

German designer Sebastian Herkner's 'Ribbon' bathroom range for Ex.t consists of a sleek console basin and bathtub. Each piece features a simple metal band (the bathtub is also available without it, as pictured). From £1,412 (ex-t.com).

SOFTLY *DOES IT*

In need of a gentler cleanse? Hansgrohe's 'Raindance' shower systems now feature the brand's 'PowderRain' technology. It provides a micro-spray that is designed to be released softly on the skin to mimic the hydrating feel of misty rain. From £170 (hansgrohe.co.uk).

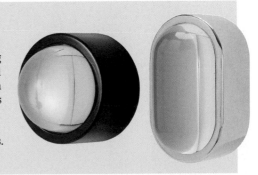

LET THERE BE LIGHTS

Your bathroom lighting options just got interesting: to coincide with the opening of his brand new headquarters, shop and restaurant in King's Cross, London, Tom Dixon has launched a series of wall lights and pendants that work in both wet and dry rooms. Choose from copper, brass, glossy black and Morwad marble finishes. From £210 (tomdixon.net).

Noir
collection by

ELLE
DECORATION

🛁 bathstore

bathstore.com/noir

Introducing Noir, an exclusive new collection by ELLE Decoration and bathstore. Dramatic industrial pieces and stunning mid-century designs, stitched together with elegant matt black metalwork, taps and fittings. Noir offers two distinct furniture designs, the caramel wood tones of Craft that you see here or the Bauhaus inspired forms of Frame. At bathstore, we pride ourselves on our expertise – proven by more than 25 years experience and 10 million satisfied customers. Noir is a beautiful new range that we are proud to introduce to the world.

TECHNOLOGY /

HOLIDAY *READ*

Airport paperbacks may be convenient, but they won't survive a dunk in the hotel swimming pool. The new Amazon 'Kindle Oasis', however, is waterproof and can last for a week on a single charge. Redesigned for easy one-handed reading, it has a seven-inch display that looks like paper, even in sunlight. Choose from a gold- or graphite-coloured case. From £229 (amazon.co.uk).

READY, JET SET, *GO!*

Before you sit on a sun terrace sipping an Italian aperitif, you'll probably have to negotiate a few planes, trains and Ubers. Thankfully, Horizn-Studios' new smart cabin suitcase, the 'Model H', can help. Its removable battery pack keeps smart devices charged and the Japanese-designed 'silent spinner' wheels help you glide effortlessly to your destination. £239 (horizn-studios.co.uk).

ELECTRIC **DREAM**

Early adopters of the electric car boom needn't compromise on style. British firm Andersen has created the 'A1' charging point in five metallic colours or Accoya wood. The 7Kw model is weatherproof with a lifetime guarantee. From £1,199 (andersen-ev.com).

VIRTUAL ASSISTANT

Looking for a stylish way to incorporate smart technology into your home? Sony's sleek 'Xperia Touch' projector turns any wall or table into a touch-sensitive 23-inch HD screen. It acts as a family hub, allowing you to leave notes, make Skype calls or view videos on YouTube. £1,400 (sony.co.uk).

LAUNDRY *SERVICE*

Stockholm-based Steamery is on a mission to make sure you always look your best. The portable 'Cirrus No.2' travel steamer heats up in 25 seconds and employs catwalk-approved technology to rejuvenate crumpled clothes. Its secret? A stainless-steel plate that spreads steam evenly to smooth out wrinkles faster. £100 (steamery.co.uk).

WORDS: TOM BAILEY

John Lewis
OF HUNGERFORD

ALFRESCO
Summer
SALE

ARCHITECTURE /

***CLOAKED HOUSE** by 3r Ernesto Pereira*
Portuguese architect Ernesto Pereira is
known for creating alluring, angular villas,
where the distinction between the interior
and the outdoors is blurred. Recently, he
completed an open-plan abode, which,
glazed on all sides, allows the surrounding
trees to form part of the décor. Raised
on stilts on a rugged hillside in Portugal's
city of Marco de Canaveses, the home
sits on a concrete base that extends out
onto a terrace, with large sliding doors.
Minimalist yet elegant in design, the
highlight of the interior is the floor-to-
ceiling windows. Punctured holes in the
concrete allow the site's existing trees to
flourish, with the lush vegetation providing
shade from the searing heat (3-r.pt).

NATURAL
HABITATIONS

*Nature is the inspiration for all three of these architectural
projects, all of which make a statement by incorporating
the surrounding landscape into their designs*

***CASA FLOTANTE** by Talleresque*
In a patch of forest at the heart of Mexico City, the
tall, narrow, three-storey Casa Flotante stands,
raised on stilts above the uneven terrain. This
home and work studio was designed by Juan De
La Rosa of architectural practice Talleresque.
The eco-friendly timber-built design, inspired
by the towering trees around it, features a mix
of Japanese and tropical influences, with sliding
doors, glazed panelling and a magnificent
wraparound staircase (talleresque.com).

***LOS TERRENOS** by Tatiana Bilbao*
Playing clever tricks on the eye, the sleek, mirrored façade of Los
Terrenos – a holiday home hidden amidst the woody terrain of
Monterrey in northeast Mexico – reflects the surrounding forest
to brilliant effect. Two large buildings surround a circular pool –
one of the structures is a rectangular block, containing the kitchen,
dining and living area, while the other houses two bedrooms.
Diamond-shaped terracotta tiles and light timber panels deck the
interior, creating a warm and welcoming space (tatianabilbao.com).

ASK AN ARCHITECT
FRIDA ESCOBEDO

We talk to the award-winning Mexican on what inspires her and the design idea behind this summer's Serpentine Pavilion

What inspired you to become an architect? I knew I wanted to do something related to the arts, but found the idea of going to Fine Arts school a bit intimidating. One week before the applications closed, I just decided to go for architecture. I became hooked, so I guess it was a good hunch.

How can architects bring value to housing design? One of the most recurrent discussions we have at the studio is the difference between exchange value and use value – some design cares too much about the former. With the support of the Sistema Nacional de Creadores (a Mexican art association that champions creativity), we are exploring how buildings that result from this lead to empty spaces in the city.

Describe your working process. We are a team of eight, and we usually discuss the initial ideas together. We start by discussing what the 'problem' of the project is – which is basically what it can express and explain to us. We then work with a lot of references, which are not necessarily architectural.

Then I try to edit as much as I can, to make it about one single, but powerful gesture. La Tallera (**4**), the art space I designed for the Chapultepec park in Mexico City, and the tilting Civic Stage (**2**), specially created for the Lisbon Triennale in 2013, are both designed for people to enjoy.

What are you working on now? Two private houses, including a mid-income project that provides the feel of living in a townhouse with a courtyard, but without the cost. Also two hotels – one in Puebla and one in Bacalar, in the Yucatán Peninsula – and a retail project in New York.

Is there a building in the world that you wish you had designed? Many, but some of them would have been impossible to be designed by a single person, such as the Mosque of Córdoba (**3**). It is a magnificent

'I like working with simple, ubiquitous materials that are often overlooked, trying to elevate them into something more profound'

piece of architecture because it has so many layers of time contained in one space.

You are the youngest architect to be commissioned for the world-famous Summer Serpentine Pavilion (1). What do you hope people will experience when entering the space? I wanted to create a design that's more contained than previous pavilions. Hyde Park is inside the city, and, by creating an interior courtyard inside the park, we would be playing with the idea of interiority and exteriority, like a Russian doll. I like working with simple and ubiquitous materials that are often overlooked, trying to elevate them into something more profound by assembling them in ways that people don't expect. In this case, we used roof tiles to create a celosia (a type of breeze-block wall). This gives the pavilion different degrees of transparency, depending on how the light hits it.

How was designing the 2015 London Design Festival installation in the iconic V&A courtyard? It was very interesting. We were commissioned to design a pavilion for the dual year between Mexico and the UK. It became a project of overlapping landscapes – both physical and cultural – similar to the idea of a mask in Greek theatre. The actor becomes the character when he puts it on, but he doesn't stop being himself. This duality was reinforced by the use of mirrored surfaces, something that would be present and also disappear by reflecting its surroundings.

If you weren't an architect, what would you be? Definitely something to do with the visual arts. *fridaescobedo.net*

WORDS: JAMES WILLIAMS. PICTURES: ANA HOP; © FRIDA ESCOBEDO/TALLER DE ARQUITECTURA; RENDERINGS BY ATMÓSFERA; CATARINA BOTELLO; GETTY; RAFAEL GAMO

THE ULTIMATE GIN & TONIC PAIRING GUIDE

Gin is only as good as the tonic it's paired with. That's why our award-winning tonic waters have been carefully crafted to complement the varied flavours of gin.

Find the perfect tonic water for your favourite gin at fever-tree.com

IF 3/4 OF YOUR DRINK IS THE MIXER, MIX WITH THE BEST™

TV when on

THE

FRAME

Art when off

Make an impression in 4K watercolour. The Frame is a stylish
4K UHD Certified TV that also allows you to marvel at your
favourite masterpieces. You'll think the Louvre's in your living room.
So whether you love romcoms or Renoir, The Frame has a mode
to make them look magnifique.

Discover how The Frame will look at home in your living room.
Visit **Samsung.com**

SAMSUNG

swoon

For the home obsessed.

ELLE
DECORATION

GLOBAL
DESIGN

THE STYLE
GUIDEBOOK

Tips from the designers behind the world's most luxurious hotels, top boutique shops to visit in major cities and a closer look at the architecture firm that's redefining glamour. Plus, the winners of the ELLE Decoration International Design Awards

The breathtaking infinity pool at Villa G in France, designed by Studio KO. To find out more about the architecture company and see more of its projects, turn to p64

HOTEL
STYLE

More than a place to stay, the best hotels are a reason to travel. Here, we look at the top designers who create that five-star feeling

Words **CLAUDIA BAILLIE**

Radisson Collection
Hotel, Royal Copenhagen

Lobby, bedroom and lounge in the 11 Howard hotel, New York

SPACE COPENHAGEN

Who are they? Signe Bindslev Henriksen and Peter Bundgaard Rützou both graduated from the Royal Danish Academy of Fine Arts school of architecture. Having started out individually, they joined forces and set up Space Copenhagen in 2005. 'Copenhagen is a small city, so as part of the same network, we knew a lot about each other,' says Henriksen. 'We were both passionate about architecture, design and materials.' Their first collaboration was a showroom for flooring company Dinesen. 'It allowed us to see whether we would benefit from working together or just kill each other!' laughs Henriksen. Luckily, the project was a success, and clients now include Fritz Hansen, Georg Jensen and Gubi.

What's their style? 'After graduation, we were part of a group who all held the same ideas; everything was minimalist with a twist. In the real world, we felt that limited our curiosity, so we began to approach things in a different way,' says Henriksen. 'We're lucky to partner with chefs, fashion designers – people who have their own creative universe.' Now, they refer to their style as 'poetic Modernism'; a contemporary design language paired with a sensitivity to the

EXPERT ADVICE

Focus on the long-term experience rather than the here and now. Trust your instincts and be honest about who you are instead of following a trend that you'll grow out of anyway.

Choose organic materials that wear well – metals, stone, wool, leather, wood. This is the only rule that has remained a constant for us, and it's how we form our colour palette. It helps to create atmosphere.

Go for things you've fallen in love with – not pieces that fit a certain style. This adds personality. We source furniture from absolutely everywhere.

Well thought out lighting is key. You can use it to completely change the look and feel of a space. Think in layers and include task lighting, as well as lamps, to create warmth. It's something we're very good at in this part of the world, as it's so dark for most of the year.

way people really live. 'Everything we create revolves around the human factor. We're always thinking about the impact space has on people,' says Rützou.

Which hotels have they designed? The duo's first major hotel project was New York's 11 Howard, located in a former Holiday Inn in the heart of Manhattan, which they completed in 2016. 'It was an interesting learning process, because we weren't able to change the configuration of the hotel's 250 rooms, which are all different. It was a huge puzzle,' says Henriksen. 'We didn't want to create a concept hotel, but wanted it to feel like home. Not necessarily Scandinavian, but with Scandinavian values in mind, and a different type of luxury from the kind you usually see in the US, which is a lot more over-the-top and bling. We wanted to create

'Our style is poetic Modernism; we want to create luxury that will still have soul in 20 years' time'

luxury that would still have soul in 20 years' time.' In order to achieve this aim, the pair introduced design pieces reminiscent of residential interiors. Instead of a chandelier, the lobby is home to a huge sculpture by Alexander Calder. The duo was also commissioned to renovate Arne Jacobsen's iconic Radisson Collection Hotel, Royal Copenhagen. 'The building's a fantastic example of Modernist architecture, so it was crucial to decide what we should preserve and what should be revitalised and brought forward to optimise the hotel's functionality,' says Henriksen.

What are they working on now? Eight hotel projects around the world, including five in Copenhagen, one in London, one in Portugal and another in Tokyo. 'The Portugal project is a 19-suite hotel in historic Porto, whereas Tokyo is a modern structure by Rem Koolhaas,' says Henriksen. 'They are all in diverse locations, and all require a very different approach.' *spacecph.dk* ➤

Hotel
Sanders,
Copenhagen

Bob & Cloche
at Gleneagles,
Scotland

Sanders
Kitchen,
Copenhagen

LIND
+ ALMOND

Who are they? Before setting up their design studio in 2015, interior designer Pernille Lind and architect Richy Almond had a significant amount of experience under their belts. Having studied at the Royal Danish Academy of Fine Arts and the University of the Arts London, Lind spent time working at Tom Dixon, Conran + Partners and Soho House, while Almond, a graduate of Northumbria University, the University of Westminster and Glasgow School of Art, had worked with Dixon Jones architects and furniture makers Based Upon. The pair met when they were both employed at Anouska Hempel Design, after which Pernille was approached to create the interior for Hotel Sanders in Copenhagen. 'We realised that it was a once in a lifetime opportunity,' she says, 'one that we felt more equipped to take on as a duo.'

What's their style? Spaces that are modern yet nostalgic. 'We use a mix of vintage and bespoke furnishings,' says Almond. 'We also come from very different backgrounds, which provides inspiration.' Half Danish and half Thai, Lind spent her childhood in her mother's antiques shop in Thailand and in a Danish family home

EXPERT ADVICE

Mix vintage with bespoke to create character. There's an abundance of good vintage shops in big cities and, of course, loads online. Invest in quality items that will last for years without going out of fashion.

One of our most important principles is to avoid trends. A good interior should be timeless, and the best are filled with things that have meaning to their owner. Don't worry about matching. A natural style will emerge over time, and the space will exude confidence.

Redecoration can happen often. It can be a small refresh or a refinement rather than a revolution.

Avoid designer lighting in favour of something simple and understated that creates a subtle wash of illumination throughout your home. In our interiors, nothing ever becomes so much of a focal point that it detracts from the rest of the space.

filled with design classics. The son of shipbuilders in northeast England, Almond grew up around the family business. 'I've always been interested in industrial design and how it can be redefined as luxurious,' he says.
Which hotels have they designed? Hotel Sanders in Copenhagen, which opened in 2017. 'Our client didn't want the hotel to feel typically Danish, so we looked outside for inspiration,' says Lind. 'We used rattan and bamboo to create a colonial feel, as well as sexy red velvet at the bar to add a touch of French chic. There's also a dose of English eccentricity and flamboyance that comes from the printed fabrics.' Danish design is referenced in the guest rooms, however, which are more pared back than the public areas. 'Although we took ideas from elsewhere, we felt a responsibility to

'We like to think of Hotel Sanders as a Danish home belonging to someone who's travelled the world'

a city renowned for its global design influence. We like to think of the hotel as a Danish home belonging to someone who's travelled the world,' adds Lind.

Also part of the duo's portfolio is Bob & Cloche, the new hair and beauty salon at the recently refurbished Gleneagles hotel, Scotland. Formerly the venue's sales office, it is now fantastically glamorous, with an Art Deco vibe, soft pastel velvets and marble.
What are they working on now? Lind runs Pernille Lind Studio, designing residential and retail projects in Denmark, while Almond heads up a team of designers and craftspeople called Novocastrian, who create bespoke furniture and installation pieces from metal and stone. 'Hotel Sanders was pretty much our dream project,' says Almond. 'To create something that will outlast ourselves was special. We'd love to continue working on hotels in interesting places, perhaps somewhere a little warmer next time.' *lindalmond.co* ➤

The conservatory
at Hotel Sanders

BRYAN O'SULLIVAN

Who is he? Having started his career in hospitality management, O'Sullivan moved into architecture via courses at the University of Greenwich and the University of Westminster, with a year spent working in the studio of New York-based architect Annabelle Selldorf. Finding himself drawn to interiors, he accepted a summer placement with the inimitable David Collins, after which he spent three years at acclaimed interior design studio Martin Brudnizki. Finally, he moved to Paris to work with French architect Luis Laplace, before setting up his own company in 2013.

What's his style? 'I have learned so much from the people I've worked with,' says O'Sullivan. 'Annabelle has a strong aesthetic, elegant with great proportions. David was super-talented and could completely change a project with the smallest tweak. Martin is equally accomplished and really knows how to bring out the best in people, and Luis taught me so much about using art and design pieces from different eras.' High on O'Sullivan's own design agenda is to make people feel at ease. 'We work hard to make even the most demanding spaces feel welcoming,' he says.

Which hotels has he designed? His biggest hospitality project to date is the Tamburlaine hotel in Cambridge, opened in 2017, which proved to be a challenging task due to the fact that the building was new. 'Everything was done off plan,' he says. 'We needed to make it feel more established, and to root the design in the city.' *The Great Tamburlaine*, a play by Cambridge's Christopher Marlowe, provided a lot of inspiration. Drawing influences from the story, O'Sullivan created a Persian garden room, as well as a timber-panelled library bar that takes its cue from the college libraries of Cambridge University. Also, there's the recently opened The Magnolia Hotel in Portugal's Quinta do Lago, an homage to the Palm Springs aesthetic.

What is he working on now? On the cusp of completion is the Stephen's Green hotel in central Dublin. 'It's in an amazing location, but hasn't been touched in 20 years. We're bringing it up to date,' says O'Sullivan. Also in the pipeline is a hotel on a golf course in Girona, Spain, with Barcelona-based GCA Architects. *bos-studio.com*

EXPERT ADVICE

Function has to come first, so plan to make sure everything physically works in a room. It's the same with choosing furniture. In the past, I've learned the hard way and chosen chairs that look incredible, but are really uncomfortable. If they're going to be used a lot, they must be comfy.

Coco Chanel once said: 'Get dressed, then take one thing off', and the same rule applies to interiors. People have a tendency to overwork things, but sometimes, simple is better.

Lighting can play a huge part in the feel of a room. When it comes to bedrooms, I prefer a central, decorative pendant light layered with small side lights and floor lamps. Downlighting can create quite a stressful space.

Tamburlaine hotel, Cambridge

'We work hard to make even the most demanding spaces feel welcoming'

The Magnolia Hotel, Quinta do Lago

The Whitby
Hotel, New York

Ham Yard
Hotel, London

Private room in
The Whitby Hotel

KIT KEMP

Who is she? Kit Kemp MBE needs no introduction. As creative director and co-owner of Firmdale Hotels, the award-winning designer has been creating unique, vibrant and inspiring interiors for almost three decades. Having trained in graphic design, she then worked for a shipping company, which allowed her to visit places such as Columbia, Guatemala and Mexico, where she collected ideas and brought back fabrics and rugs. Next, she worked for Polish architect Leszek Nowicki,

> 'The whole look of a hotel should be an adventure for the senses. Most importantly, though, it should make people smile'

who became a huge influence. It was, in fact, Nowicki who first introduced her to Tim Kemp, her now husband and co-owner of the Firmdale group. 'He was a developer and was upgrading some of his properties,' explains Kemp. 'He'd been working on hotels offering student accommodation, so we decided to do something different and have a go at creating a small boutique place together.' As well as stylish hotels, Kit also designs textiles, fragrances and homewares, and has written two interior design books.

What's her style? 'I'm always looking for ideas wherever I go,' says Kemp. 'Private homes, museums and art galleries all inspire me, but my biggest thing is textiles – remnants, colourful threads, ethnic, ancient, contemporary, colourful or monotone. I love colour, and I like my interiors to look carefree.' Organic, natural pieces play a big part in her work, as does travel. A sense of discovery through each space is important, as is having a clear identity for every project. 'I look at everything afresh. Obviously interiors will display our signature, but they should be of this moment, not of yesterday's moment. With good design, you

shouldn't be able to imagine it from the start – it should become larger than your original idea,' she says. 'The key is to always be curious. The whole look of a hotel should be an adventure for the senses. Most importantly, though, it should make people smile.'

Which hotels has she designed? Kemp's first hotel, Dorset Square, opened in London in 1985. 'It was really great fun working on the design, even though I had no formal training,' she says. 'I meet people now and they say, "When I've done my design course", or when I've done this and that, but sometimes, you've just got to get on and do it!' Since then, along with husband Tim, Kemp has expanded her portfolio to include no fewer than ten properties in both London and New York, including the Covent Garden Hotel, the Charlotte Street Hotel, the Soho Hotel, Ham Yard and her most recent hotel project, The Whitby in upper midtown Manhattan, which opened to the public in February 2017.

What is she working on now? Although there are no more hotels on the horizon at the moment, Kemp is always working on her next big project. A third interior design book is due for release in April 2019, while a second collection of china with Wedgwood, called 'Sailor's Farewell', will be out later this year, as will an exciting new wallpaper and fabric collection for Andrew Martin. *firmdalehotels.com* ➤

EXPERT ADVICE

Don't just use wallpaper on walls. Fabric can add texture and warmth to your home, and gives a cosy but tailored look.

If you make a collection of something, it becomes interesting. We collect meat platters at The Whitby and bowling shoes in the bowling alley at Ham Yard. Framed in Perspex boxes, with a black felt background, they become works of art in themselves.

Colours don't have to match. If they complement each other it's more interesting. I'll often have a plain wall, then introduce one large pattern alongside smaller ones, so that they're not competing. Breaking the rules and stretching the imagination is fun.

A small detail can provide the lyrical element that brings a whole room to life. Look for unusual fabrics with something that captures your imagination. They will be the thing people always remember.

PICTURES: SIMON BROWN

Kimpton Rowan,
Palm Springs

Kimpton De Witt,
Amsterdam

Wyers Bar at
Kimpton De Witt

AVE BRADLEY

Who is she? Bradley's first foray into design began on the sales floor at American furniture store Pottery Barn, where she worked her way up to become a furniture buyer. Thanks to two former colleagues who were chosen to lead the W Hotels launch in 1998, she was asked to join the newly formed design team. 'Nobody came from a hospitality background, and I froze at the importance of it all. I had to dig deep or return to something comfortable – it was a choice that would define me.' As director of interiors and brand development, she worked on the group's first 24 hotels over the course of six years, after which she set up her own hospitality design consulting business, Fishnet Holdings. A project with a client who was planning a Kimpton hotel led to her joining the boutique hotel brand in 2009 as vice president of design, where she has since spearheaded its projects across the US.

What's her style? 'Things differ a lot from hotel to hotel, but ultimately, it's all about creating a sense of style and fun for the guests,' says Bradley. 'It's important to research. I like to move through each city, to understand as much of the culture as possible, then elements can be

EXPERT ADVICE
I like to build up what I call an 'envelope' of timeless materials and finishes that can serve as a beautiful blank canvas for the rest of the furnishings to be layered on top of. This way, the scheme will have a grounding that can endure over several small, less challenging refreshes.

Learning to edit your belongings is a great skill to develop. When you gain a bit of space in a room, there's more opportunity to appreciate each object, piece of furniture or artwork.

Be willing to have some fun and add a piece of art, a cushion or a feature chair that's in complete contrast to the aesthetic in the rest of your home.

Allow your space to be a personal reflection of your journeys and adventures. Bring in inspiring books, an object that you found that triggers a moment seared into your memory, or sentimental things that remind you of a magical time in your life.

incorporated into the design. Guests are curious to understand local environments, and I want our hotels to be authentically connected and embraced by the community.' Because of often strict architecture and material palettes, Bradley's aim is to soften each space in order to stop it feeling like a museum. 'The key is to avoid having everything matching,' she says. 'Perfection is boring, so I always find ways to add something offbeat or unexpected. That can be a fantastic statement piece – found furniture, a custom-designed element or a significant artwork – or, of course, beautiful styling.'

Which hotels has she designed? As well as an impressive portfolio of hotels, bars and restaurants across the US – including 24 for the W Group, five with Fishnet Holdings and more than 75 so far for Kimpton – Bradley has recently overseen the design of the Kimpton De Witt, the brand's first European hotel, which opened in Amsterdam in May 2017. Marrying two modern structures and three original buildings from the Dutch Golden Age, the hotel is designed to honour its heritage, while adding a sense of joy. A living wall graces the entrance, while bedrooms feature many memorable touches, such as humorous interpretations of classic Dutch art, beautiful bedside lamps featuring birds by Atelier Areti and porcelain parrot statues by Dutch designer Pols Potten. Work by local and international artists is displayed throughout, and the hotel even has its own flower shop.

What is she working on now? Bradley is currently overseeing the design of the forthcoming Kimpton Paris, due for completion in 2020. 'It's hard to imagine anything more interesting, challenging and exciting than to open a hotel in Paris,' she says. 'It's one of the true capitals of fashion and style, so I hope to do it justice.' Also in the pipeline is the Saint George Hotel in Toronto, opening this summer, while further Kimpton venues are scheduled to launch in Taipei, Bali, Hainan Island, Shanghai, London, Manchester and Edinburgh before 2021. *kimptonhotels.com* ED

PICTURES: CHRIS GUILLEN, LAURIE JOLIET

'The key is to avoid having everything matching. Perfection is boring, so I always find a way to add something offbeat or unexpected'

Window Bar at Kimpton Rowan

ARCHITECTS
OF PARADISE

The creative talent behind many of the world's most envy-enducing
buildings, Studio KO is a firm synonymous with international glamour

Words **TOM DELAVAN AND JULIEN GUIEU**
Photography **DAN GLASSER**

Olivier Marty and Karl Fournier, the duo behind the Paris-based architecture firm Studio KO, have accomplished much in their twenty-year partnership, which began when they met as students in 1996. Their projects are grounded in humility, collaboration and deference – to context, to history and to their clients. 'Carte blanche is the death of everything,' declares Marty, dismissing the popular idea that the best work comes from an aggressively singular vision, unchallenged by circumstance. 'We like to think about the best solution to the problem, and not impose our own language.'

Such an approach means Studio KO intentionally avoids a signature look. 'We wish for there to be no KO style, but a KO attitude,' says Fournier. Indeed, rather than seeing the precise requirements of a client as an impediment, they see them as essential to their work. One can scarcely believe that the same firm is behind the Villa E in Morocco (overleaf), a monolithic and quietly powerful building, and the Edwardian-style Chiltern Firehouse hotel in London. There is modesty even in the culturally rooted materials that Studio KO favours: stone, dry earth, rough-hewn beams. 'We don't like sleek,' says Marty. 'We prefer things that show they've been crafted by someone's hands.' Here, we look at some of the duo's most exciting builds, featured in recent book *Studio KO* (£55, Rizzoli). *studioko.fr*

VILLA K, *MOROCCO*

Perched atop a long rocky strip of land, this house's garden level, located below the main floor, closely hugs the local terrain. After climbing the outdoor stairs, you arrive at a jutting infinity pool that reaches out to the distant mountains. Almost perpendicular to the pool, the floor-to-ceiling windows allow a panoramic view, with the interior protected from the Moroccan sun by a steel-and-cedar-wood awning, which creates streaks of shade that penetrate deep into the house. ➤

VILLA G, *FRANCE*

A concrete parallelepiped (or rhomboid), this house appears to levitate over a hillside in southern France, in bold defiance of gravity. Cantilevered on either side of a minimal garden, the villa's uncluttered interior asserts itself with clarity. In its centre, a wooden volume gathers together all of the utilitarian areas of the home, from the kitchen to the bathroom. On either side of this core, the living room and bedroom unfurl with ample dimensions and wide windows that allow your gaze to take flight across the rural landscape.

VILLA E, *MOROCCO*

Behind a heavy metal door, this home has a soft, airy interior that contrasts with the roughness of its façade – much as the house's sharp, angular edges stand out against the curves of the surrounding countryside. The living room resembles a movie theatre in which the screen has been replaced by a window of cinematic proportions. It offers a perfectly framed view of Jebel Toubkal, the highest peak in the Atlas Mountains. ➤

YVES SAINT LAURENT MUSEUM, *MOROCCO*

To protect the Fondation Pierre Bergé – Yves Saint Laurent's couture collections, Studio KO had to design a building to keep the potentially damaging rays of the sun at bay. Its exhibition galleries, conservation areas and auditoriums are largely windowless by necessity. The interior is smooth and shimmering, while the outside seems woven and colourful. **ED**

DESIGN DESTINATIONS

No holiday is complete without a big shopping spree. So, wherever you're jetting off to this summer, we reveal the best interiors boutiques to visit Words **EMMA LOVE**

MAGAZYN ANTWERP

Arranged in rooms to echo the layout of an open-plan home, Magazyn sells a curated range of high-end, handcrafted pieces from around the world: think oversized bowls from Cambodia, Austrian glassware and Italian linens. Founder, creative director and interior designer Thomas Haarmann's own collection of grey, minimalist furniture and accessories is a highlight. His message: buy less, buy meaningful. *magazyn.be*

BUNGALOW 8 MUMBAI

Now as much about fashion as interiors, this Mumbai shopping institution is tucked under the bleachers of the Wankhede cricket stadium. Founder Maithili Ahluwalia shines a spotlight on Indian design, sourcing many of her objects – from a painted bench to silver spoons and ornate mirrors – from local stately homes. There's always something unusual to discover. *bungaloweight.com*

ONORA MEXICO CITY

Located in the upscale neighbourhood of Polanco, this four-year-old shop is a platform for contemporary Mexican textiles and homeware. The aim of its designer founders, Maria Eladia Hagerman and Maggie Galton, is to present traditional craft techniques using a modern, muted colour palette. Each piece is created in collaboration with artisans: expect cotton and alpaca pillows produced on backstrap looms by Tzotzil-speaking weavers from the highlands of Chiapas and lacquered bowls made by the Nahua community in the state of Guerrero. *onoracasa.com*

BILLIE ROSE GHENT

Owned by brother and sister duo Noor and Wolf Callebaut (she looks after the shop, he runs the café), this new concept store sells homeware by up-and-coming makers that you're unlikely to find elsewhere. Named after Noor's daughter, the exterior has a black criss-cross façade, while inside, the look is pale and interesting, with blush pink walls. Find limited-edition lamps by Ghent-based photographer Luca Bell (from a collaboration with cool lifestyle brand LRNCE), vases by Hear Hear and vessels by Ginger Ceramics. Plus, there are blankets by Forestry Wool and soy candles by Brandt Kaarsen, both brands from nearby Utrecht. *billierose.be*

ARTILLERIET GOTHENBURG

From the clusters of vases and candlesticks artfully arranged on dining tables to a glass cabinet filled with trinkets, this Swedish shop is a treasure trove of eclectic pieces by brands such as Astier de Villatte, Muuto, Society Limonta and John Derian. Every item is hand-picked by founders Christian Divenvoorden and Sofie Hellsing, who opened Artilleriet seven years ago. In 2014, the duo expanded into the shop next door with the launch of Artilleriet The Kitchen, a space dedicated to selling beautiful glassware, cutlery, tableware and more. *artilleriet.se*

TONIC DESIGN JOHANNESBURG

An architectural design studio founded by friends Greg Gamble and Philippe van der Merwe, Tonic Design specialises in contemporary custom-made and limited-edition furniture and accessories. Sitting alongside its own collections in the showroom are pieces by international brands, such as ClassiCon, Gubi and Jieldé, plus displays of specially commissioned artworks, ceramics and glass by South African artisans. This summer, the duo are launching their biggest range of furniture yet, including sofas, armchairs, tables and storage units made from timber, steel and natural stone. *tonicdesign.co.za* ➤

PICTURES: RAOUL BAJAJ, JAIME NAVARRO

SPARTAN PORTLAND

After founding Spartan ten years ago in Austin, Texas, Currie Person and her husband moved across America and re-opened their shop in Portland, Oregon at the end of 2016. Much of what's for sale is made in the US, whether it's furniture by LA-based brother-and-sister brand De Jong & Co, lighting by local Portland multidisciplinary studio ParkerWorks or custom-designed glass Champagne flutes by Esque Studio (also from Portland). The shop is equally well known for its range of ceramics by the likes of Eric Bonnin, Lilith Rockett and Kati Von Lehman, and its sell-out art shows – the quiet, artisanal feel of the store makes it an ideal gallery space. *spartan-shop.com*

THE HUB GENERAL STORE MELBOURNE

After years spent happily browsing flea markets, Jacqueline Foti-Lowe (founder of Hub Furniture, a long-established Melbourne design showroom selling furniture, lighting and home accessories) decided to dedicate a new space to championing everyday objects. The shop, which opened at the end of last year, sells vintage and handmade goods, as well as useful items, such as Merchant & Mills sewing kits. *thehubgeneralstore.com.au*

IITTALA AND ARABIA DESIGN CENTRE HELSINKI

This unique venue brings together classic and limited-edition pieces by two of Finland's most celebrated design brands: Iittala and Arabia. Housed in the former factory where Arabia's products were once made, it's part museum, part shop, so you can learn about the history of glass and ceramics (don't miss iconic works by design legends Tapio Wirkkala and Kaj Franck) before heading to the second floor to spend some money. Top buys include Alvar Aalto vases, jewel-hued Kastehelmi tumblers and Iittala mugs, with surrealist illustrations by the likes of Ugo Gattoni and Merijn Hos. *designcentrehelsinki.com*

KOLLEKTED BY OSLO

Interior stylists Jannicke Kråkvik and Alessandro D'Orazio felt like something was missing from Oslo's shopping streets, so in 2013, they opened Kollected By. Now located in a former butchers, the store is the only Norwegian retailer to stock furniture and homeware by Copenhagen-based brand Frama. Also look out for ceramics by Tina Marie and Anette Krogstad (she's made tableware for the new Noma 2.0 restaurant). *kollektedby.no*

EMPREINTES PARIS

Opened in 2016 by Ateliers d'Art de France, a trade union for craftspeople, to showcase the work of French artisans, this is a one-of-a-kind shop. There are more than 1,000 pieces on display, from gorgeous goblets and vases by Marie Verlet to grey felt cushions by Ghislaine Garcin, and forged knives in olive wood by Maurice Dubost. On the top floor, there's a book shop specialising in art and design tomes, while in the basement, you'll find a screening room showing craft-related films. *empreintes-paris.com*

SIRIN COPENHAGEN

Named after Russian-American novelist Vladimir Nabokov, whose pen surname was Sirin, this Danish store is owned by Natalia Enge, who is constantly on the lookout for work by interesting emerging designers. Her latest discoveries include Australia-born, Copenhagen-based Nikolai Kotlarczyk's baroque-inspired brass mirrors, as well as local brand Moebe, whose shelving will be available in-store soon. *sirincopenhagen.com*

STAHL + BAND LOS ANGELES

Part showroom, part gallery, this shop is housed in the former studio of the late actor Dennis Hopper, near Venice Beach. Its name, which translates from German as 'steel and ribbon', is an homage to owner Jeffery Molter's ancestry and the work of his favourite artist, Richard Serra. Inside, over half of what's on show – wicker bar stools, a steel-framed sofa, an ash dining table – is designed by Molter, but there are also limited-edition natural rush benches by artist David McAuliffe and cast-glass bowls by Steven Haulenbeek. *stahlandband.com* ED

NEW
DESIGN
CLASSICS

The ELLE Decoration International Design Awards – this year held in partnership with boutique hotel brand MGallery – shine a light on the world's best new furniture, lighting, tableware and more. Voted by us, as well as our 24 fellow editions around the globe, this is the definitive edit of what's hot in 2018

Photography **ANDREA GARUTI**
Styling **ELISA OSSINO STUDIO**
Words **PAOLA CARIMATI**

SEATING 'FIL NOIR' BY CHRISTOPHE DELCOURT FOR MINOTTI

This project is built around the concept of a thread (or *fil* in French, giving this chair its name), a design feature that is a metaphor for continuity. Here, the thread takes the form of black metal tubing, which not only outlines the piece's silhouette, but supports and envelops it. From gorgeous, putty-coloured upholstery to perfectly soft goose-down filling, all of the materials for this design have been meticulously selected. This great attention to detail, craftsmanship and sophisticated yet simple style is what sets the 'Fil Noir' apart. £4,825 (minottilondon.com).

BATHROOM 'IMMERSION'
BY NERI & HU FOR AGAPE

The first bathroom project from this Chinese design practice, Neri & Hu's 'Immersion' bathtub was created to answer the needs of younger generations who tend to live in smaller apartments. The tub makes new use of a traditional design to get around the issue of space, following in the footsteps of soaking tubs, popular in Japan. Deep rather than wide, it provides a perfectly relaxing experience and, with its minimal lines, stylishly updates an ancient idea for contemporary living. £7,080 (agapedesign.it).

FABRIC 'TRUE VELVET' COLLECTION
BY INDIA MAHDAVI FOR PIERRE FREY

'After decades of beige and white, colour is dressing our living rooms,' declares Mahdavi – referred to as the 'queen of colour' – who, with this collection of velvets, intends to create joy. The designer's passion for brights can be traced back to her Iranian-Egyptian culture and cosmopolitan childhood (born in Tehran, she grew up in the US, Germany and France). Pick from two prints, one with a diamond pattern (below) and one striped, both in a choice of 80 colours. £223.20 per metre (pierrefrey.com).

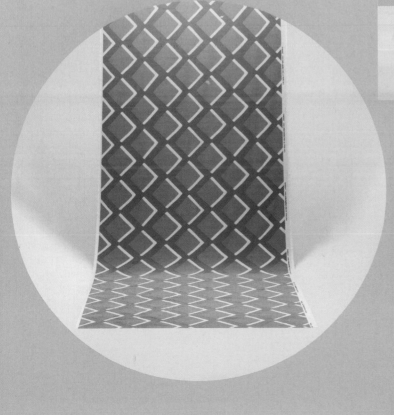

YOUNG DESIGNER
STUDIO SWINE

This collaboration between Japanese architect Azusa Murakami and British artist Alexander Groves has a uniquely broad approach and style, with work straddling the spheres of art, design and cinema. Indeed, the studio's very name is a mission statement – Swine stands for 'Super Wide Interdisciplinary New Explorers'. One of its most enchanting projects is 'New Spring' – produced for fashion brand Cos and shown at last year's Milan Furniture Fair, it consisted of a stylised white aluminium tree that produced steam-filled soap bubbles that burst on contact with the human body. The concept was inspired by the cherry blossom festival in Japan and, like many of Studio Swine's other works, it pays homage to experiential art and collective participation (studioswine.com). ➤

OUTDOOR 'MANILA' CHAIR BY PAOLA NAVONE FOR BAXTER

With a slender structure and an exotic silhouette, this outdoor chair by Italian designer Navone is designed to bring glamour to gardens. A large part of its visual strength is thanks to its hand-picked materials – manila reed tubing (which gives the project its name), oxidised copper for the frame, and leather-wrapped technical cord for the woven seat. In order to protect the chair from the elements, a special leather tanning technique and Indian ink dye have been used, which limit the ageing and fading caused by UV rays. This extra protection ensures this design will last many summers. £7,056, Silvera (silveraltd.co.uk; baxter.it).

BEDDING 'WINGS' BED BY JAIME HAYÓN FOR WITTMANN

Is it a bird? Is it a bed? The focus of this design by creative Spanish designer Hayón is its adjustable upholstered wings. When folded in, they turn the bed into a cosy cocoon, the perfect place for a dreamy night's sleep. When open, the wings create a striking profile. It is this ability to alter the mood – to create intimacy or exuberance – that makes this such an interesting piece of design. The built-in bedside tables are covered in luxe leather and equipped with LED lamps that are perfect for some bedtime reading. From £15,869 (wittmann.at).

ELLE
DECORATION
BRITISH DESIGN AWARDS

2018

Once again, this September we will be saluting the very best of British design talent across 13 different categories. For more details and information on how you can make your own nominations, visit elledecoration.co.uk

Chelford Dove Grey from the Shaker collection

www.howdens.com
or call 0800 0639 290 to request a brochure

HILLARYS

You'll love what we do

BLINDS | CURTAINS | SHUTTERS | CARPETS

MEASURED AND FITTED FOR YOU

VISIT HILLARYS.CO.UK

#ILOVETHATSTYLE

HOWDENS
JOINERY CO.

MAKING SPACE MORE VALUABLE

HILLARYS

You'll love what we do

BLINDS | CURTAINS | SHUTTERS | CARPETS

MEASURED AND FITTED FOR YOU

VISIT HILLARYS.CO.UK

#ILOVETHATSTYLE

ELLE DECORATION
HOMES

VENICE / BALI / PONZA / WAIHEKE ISLAND / SORRENTO / LITTLE KAROO

HOLIDAY IN STYLE

*Blue skies, hot sun and stunning interiors...
This month's homes are the ultimate summer
destinations – and you can book a stay in
all of them. It's time to upgrade your vacation*

ISLAND LIFE

With its palette of dazzling whites and cool blues,
this Italian holiday home is a haven of tranquillity

Words **CLAUDIA BAILLIE**

Photography **ALESSANDRA IANNIELLO/LIVING INSIDE**

Off the west coast of Italy, in the sparkling Tyrrhenian sea, you'll find Ponza, the largest of the Pontine Islands. It was in this picturesque spot – with its labyrinth of grottoes, talcum powder beaches and pirate caves – that artist Mita Ungaro Vicario spent much of her childhood. 'Before we bought this holiday home, I hadn't been back for over 20 years,' she says. 'When I first returned, I burst into tears.'

Carved into the cliffs overlooking the water, the cavernous space was once used by locals as a place to store supplies, after which it was transformed into an elegant house by its previous owner, a Roman architect. But it wasn't until after that emotional visit that Mita and her husband, Stefano, discovered the hidden gem while exploring the island with an old friend. 'The house had appeared to my husband in a dream,' explains Mita. 'He immediately recognised it. Our friend knew the owner and put us in touch. Finally, after a year of trying to persuade him, he agreed to sell.'

Despite its inherent charm, the two-bedroomed home had lain abandoned for many years, so there was plenty of work to be done. The biggest surprise was the incredible floor, made up of handmade 18th-century Riggiole Napoletane tiles. 'We found them under a thick layer of sand, so we cleaned them up and added more,' says Mita. One of the only decorative elements in the house, the tiles work perfectly with its whitewashed walls and minimal interior, where much of the furniture is integrated into the very fabric of the building. Linens by Society Limonta and ceramics bought from Le Cose Di Mari, Mita's favourite island store, add the only other splashes of colour.

Perhaps the most impressive area in this home is the breathtaking terrace. 'It's the best spot to enjoy the sunrise or the full moon, or to watch the boats passing by,' says Mita. 'We love the pure air, the view and the peaceful location. This is an enchanted place to stay with loved ones, or anyone I welcome as my guest.'

HOW TO BOOK Ferries to Ponza from Anzio on the mainland take an hour and 20 minutes. Villa Mita sleeps up to eight people, with three bedrooms. Prices start at £439 per night. Head to homesineataly.com

Seating areas and stairs are carved into the soft, sculptural curves of the interior. Upholstery and cushions add comfort, and treasures from the sea are displayed on the built-in shelves ➤

THE MOODBOARD

The airy, summery look of this home is achieved using natural textures and a palette of blue and white

1 'Pure White' **paint**, £44 for 2.5 litres, Designers Guild (designersguild.com) **2** 'Perfect White' **paint**, £53 for 2.5 litres, Zoffany (stylelibrary.com/zoffany)
3 'Azure Blue' **tile**, £3.25 each, Bert & May (bertandmay.com) **4** 'Acapulco' **tile** in 'Alva', £375.06 per square metre, Fired Earth (firedearth.com) **5** 'Narrow Stripe'
linen in 'Sea Green/White', £38 per metre, Volga Linen (volgalinen.co.uk) **6** 'Blue Siham' **metro-style tile**, £1 each, Bert & May (bertandmay.com) **7** 'Stripes'
soup plate, £9.95, Liberty (libertylondon.com) **8** 'Cannes Mae' **tile**, £579.78 per square metre, Claybrook (claybrookstudio.co.uk) **9** 'Caribbean Blue' **zellige tile**,
£150 per square metre, Terrazzo Tiles (terrazzo-tiles.co.uk) **10** 'Tangier' **tile**, £3.84 each, Artisans of Devizes (artisansofdevizes.com) **11** Set of **carafe and glass**,
£70, Liberty (libertylondon.com) **12** 'Ohio' **fabric**, £117.60 per metre, Pierre Frey (pierrefrey.com) **13** Olivewood **board**, £17.25, Divertimenti (divertimenti.co.uk)
14 Echiveria **plant**, from £3; **pot**, £3, both Botany (botanyshop.co.uk) **15** 'La Maison' **tile**, £54 per square metre, Mandarin Stone (mandarinstone.com)
16 'Acapulco' **tile** in 'Yellow City', £64.98 per square metre, Fired Earth (firedearth.com) **17** Pre-assembled **tile panel**, £201.60 per square metre, Habibi
(habibi-interiors.com) **18** 'Linara' **linen** in 'Rose Quartz', £38.50 per metre, Romo (romo.com) **19** **Basket** by Makaua, £18, The Conran Shop (conranshop.co.uk) ➤

'We found the 18th-century *Riggiole Napoletane* tiles under a thick layer of sand, so we cleaned them up and *added more*'

Kitchen The Riggiole Napoletane tiles are an original feature, produced in Naples in the 1700s **Bathroom** Original black and brown tiles decorate the floor. An Indian teak mirror hangs above the simple ceramic basin ➤

Terrace With its breathtaking view, this is homeowner Mita's (right) favourite part of the house. A reed canopy provides shade during the sunniest parts of the day. The wooden outdoor table was found in the house and painted light blue to mimic the colour of the sea ➤

'The *house* had appeared
    to my husband in a dream.
It was *astonishing*,
        with such a *poetic* beauty'

Bedrooms These spaces
are made intimate thanks
to the enveloping cave
walls. Graphic floor tiles
add a hit of decoration,
and the bedlinens are by
Society Limonta **Stockist
details on p167** ED

ART & SOUL

This living art gallery on Venice's Grand Canal retains all of its mid-century grandeur

Words **JAMES RICH** Photography **HELENIO BARBETTA/LIVING INSIDE** Styling **CHIARA DAL CANTO**

Entrance With its walls covered in mustard-coloured marmorino (a kind of polished plaster), the entrance to the property is as much an art showcase as a vestibule. The ceramic and glass console is by Marcello Fantoni, and is home to a 1920s Murano glass plate and vase ➤

C linging to the banks of Venice's Grand Canal, and basking in the reflected glory of the Palazzo Venier dei Leoni opposite, sits the home of Australian art collector Nikki McCullagh and her husband Paul. Despite its arched windows and 18th-century frontage, this is no ordinary Venetian dwelling. Once home to another art collector, the famed Peggy Guggenheim, the opulent, three-bedroomed property is now a space that's been specifically designed for showcasing artworks, with two huge living rooms and a Modernist dining room.

'When I was looking to buy, I saw all sorts of houses that were steeped in history and atmosphere,' recalls Nikki. 'But here, the canal views are extraordinary, as mesmerising as a Caravaggio painting.' With so many different viewpoints from the house – the garden of the Casetta Rossa, a much-loved little red palazzo on the canal's edge, can also be seen to the east – 'you feel as though you're on a boat, floating through the city centre,' says Nikki.

She and Paul commissioned architectural studio Ta Architettura – which specialises in the restoration of period properties in Venice – and Parisian interior designer Jacques Grange to work on the space. 'It was immediately clear that the main appeal of this home was its natural light and its relationship with the outdoors,' remembers Nikki. 'We wanted the architecture itself to be the protagonist – to take the leading role in the look and feel of the property.'

To that end, almost all of the doors were removed, opening up passages between the mustard-coloured marmorino plaster walls of the entrance and allowing it to glow in the light that trickles in. The original terrazzo floors were restored – 'and are lovely to walk on; cool, like marble,' says Nikki – while bronze was used for the kitchen furniture. The décor was purposefully kept uncluttered so as not to overshadow the views of the city. 'We treated each window as a portal that would bring the beauty of Venice inside,' explains Nikki. 'Like works of art in themselves, they punctuate the space.' *taarchitettura.com*

HOW TO BOOK The house is a 20-minute car journey from Venice's Marco Polo Airport. Book for up to six people, at £1,321 per night, with a minimum stay of three nights, at veniceprestige.com

Opposite The smaller of the two living rooms is structured around a view of the Gritti Palace through its mullioned windows. The brown velvet lounge chair is by Gio Ponti, while the blue armchairs are vintage Italian pieces from the 1940s. The 'Leaves' chandelier is by Angelo Lelli for Arredoluce from SG Gallery in Milan **Stockist details on p167** ➤

Kitchen The table is by Swiss designer Jurg Bally, paired with 'Superleggera' chairs by Gio Ponti for Cassina
Main living room 'Digamma' armchairs by Ignazio Gardella for Santa & Cole face the window. The coffee table
is also by Ignazio Gardella for Azucena. The artwork is *Untitled* by Michael Goldberg **Stockist details on p167 ➤**

Main living room On the table sits the 'Spaziale' vase by Antonia Campi for Nape' Venezia. The 'Library' shelving along the wall is by Ignazio Gardella **Dining room** The 'Pietra Serena' table is by Angelo Mangiarotti, the 'Luisa' chairs are by Franco Albini for Cassina and the 'LS2' lights are by Luigi Caccia Dominioni for Azucena **Stockist details on p167** ➤

Bathroom Impressive swathes of Zebrino marble envelop this space, with bronze 'Tara' taps by Dornbracht. The bathtub itself is coated in Cremo Tirreno marble **Opposite** A sleek black basin, along with another set of 'Tara' taps, adds a luxurious touch to the guest bathroom **Stockist details on p167 ➤**

Bedroom A majestic four poster bed rests beneath the ceiling's original vaulted beams. The 'TL2' writing desk is by Franco Albini for Poggi, and the Italian armchairs are from the 1950s. Hanging on the wall is *Diamond Dust Shoes*, an artwork by Andy Warhol **Stockist details on p167** ED

'WATCHING THE LIGHT FALL THROUGH TREE BRANCHES ONTO THE HOUSE REALLY IS THE MOST BEAUTIFUL THING'

The owners of this minimal Balinese haven have created a home in which it's impossible not to feel the calming effects of the rainforest

Words **JAMES CUNNINGHAM**
Photography **KARINA TENGBERG/HOUSE OF PICTURES**
Production **TAMI CHRISTIANSEN/HOUSE OF PICTURES**

Exterior Raised above the forest floor, this large decked area has amazing panoramic views. The swimming pool is essential for cooling down in the Balinese heat ➤

A

bundant and lush native greenery surrounds Origami
House, one of a cluster of new homes to have been built
in the small village of Mas, where artists, musicians and
yoga experts have established the Penjiwaan community.
A destination for wellness and meditation, the area is just
ten minutes from Ubud, the island's cultural hub.

Designed by Bali-based architect Alexis Dornier for
German couple Johannes and Stefanie Strachwitz, this
home gets its name from the dynamic structure of its
angular timber roof, which encourages the flow of air
through the property. Blending architectural influences
from East and West, the overall effect is contemporary
and timeless, with each space having its own identity
while also feeling open to the elements – 'it's like a village
in a house,' says Alexis. Materials have been sourced
locally, while much of the furniture has been designed
and produced by makers from the region.

'We wanted no transition between inside and out,'
explain Johannes and Stefanie, who welcome in the vivid
views with double-height windows and panoramic, wraparound terraces. 'Watching the light of the rainforest fall
though the tree branches onto the house really is the most
beautiful thing,' the couple say. The sprawling palms that
enclose the house also afford it a significant level of privacy,
shielding the home from its neighbours in the community.

'Being surrounded by greenery is the biggest luxury we
can have as humans,' say Johannes and Stefanie, paying
further homage to the natural splendour that makes
Origami House such a special place. *alexisdornier.com*

HOW TO BOOK Transfers from Bali's Denpasar
Airport take around an hour by car, and can be arranged
when booking. Origami House sleeps eight people, with four
bedrooms and four bathrooms. Prices start at £350 per night,
with a minimum stay of four nights. To enquire about available
dates, email ubudorigamihouse@gmail.com

Dining area The table and chairs are made by local craftspeople and the 'HL-03' pendant lights come from Vio Gallery in nearby Ubud. Designer Jonas Ruf crafted the bespoke kitchen island from a fallen tree found in the rainforest **Stockist details on p167 ➤**

Living area This recessed space features a sofa made to order by Bianco Interior, a local design firm. The rugs are from nearby Seminyak
Hallway The 'Hardoy Chair' by Jorge Ferrari Hardoy, sold by Knoll, has an enviable vantage point
Stockist details on p167 ➤

ORIGAMI
HOUSE GETS
ITS NAME
FROM THE
DYNAMIC
STRUCTURE OF
ITS ANGULAR
TIMBER ROOF

Bedroom With a pared-back style and direct access to a decked area, this is a space for maximum relaxation. The bedlinen was all handmade by a local artisan –for similar, try Piglet **Bathroom** The outdoor tub, just visible from the bedroom, was bought at a local store on the outskirts of Ubud **Stockist details on p167** ED

ATTENTION
HAS BEEN
PAID TO
SOURCING
MATERIALS
AND PIECES
OF FURNITURE
LOCALLY

From left 'Orson' **deckchair** by Gordon Guillaumier, £1,035, Roda (rodaonline.com). 'Havana' **rug** in 'Curry', from £1,414, Élitis (elitis.fr). 'Composizione 57 10' **patterned rug** by Manlio Rho, £8,989, Amini Carpets (amini.it). 'Pageant' **fabric**, £120 per metre, Osborne & Little (osborneandlittle.com). 'Esedra' round **coffee table** by Luca Nichetto for Ethimo, from £480, Houseology (houseology.com). **Small vase** and **ceramic object**, from a selection at Officine Saffi (officinesaffi.com). 'Masai' **striped vase**, from £167, Serena Confalonieri (serenaconfalonieri.com). 'Brixx' **sofa** by Lorenza Bozzoli, £3,150. Dedon (dedon.de). 'Bliss Wall' **rug** **(on wall)** by Mae Engelgeer, £1,357 per square metre, CC-Tapis (cc-tapis.com). 'Modena' **pendant light** by Area-17, £595, Martinelli Luce (martinelliluce.it) ➤

FEEL THE HEAT

Set the scene for summer days, with bold African-inspired prints and intense, saturated colour

Photography **ANDREA GARUTI**

Styling **ARIANNA LELLI MAMI AND CHIARA DI PINTO/STUDIOPEPE**

From left 'Matera' **side table** by Paola Navone for Baxter, £4,385, Silvera (silveraltd.co.uk). 'Traveler' **outdoor armchair with hood** by Stephen Burks, £2,440, Roche Bobois (roche-bobois.com). 'Mbrace' **rocking chair**, £1,650; **footrest**, £600, both by Sebastian Herkner for Dedon (dedon.de). 'Opera' **mirror**, £291, Élitis (elitis.fr). 'Garden Layers' **padded rugs** by Patricia Urquiola, from £305, Gan Rugs (gan-rugs.com). 'Soho' **pendant light** by Joan Gaspar for Marset, £505, Twentytwentyone (twentytwentyone.com). 'Architecture 2' **tapestry**, £1,696, Nicolette Brunklaus (nicolettebrunklaus.com). 'Geometric Pic Nic' embroidered hessian **fabric**, £167.50 per square metre, Dedar (dedar.com). 'Nar 53' **chair** by Louis Benech, £849, Royal Botania (royalbotania.com) ➤

From left 'Ginestra' **outdoor chair** by Antonio Citterio, £1,063, B&B Italia (bebitalia.com). 'Asterias' **table** by Patricia Urquiola, from £4,873, Molteni & C (molteni.it). Two 'Masai' **vases**, as before. 'Vasum' **bowl** by Maria Gabriella Zecca, £378, Tacchini Edizione (tacchini.it). 'Bon Ton' **pendant light** by Cristina Celestino for Torremato, £390, The Conran Shop (conranshop.co.uk). 'Havana' **rug**, as before. 'Flutti' **green rug**, £9,347, Paola Lenti (paolalenti.it). 'Esedra' **sofa** by Luca Nichetto for Ethimo, from £4,064, Houseology (houseology.com). 'Fizz' **small cushion**, £83; 'Bubble' **larger cushion**, £113.80, both Élitis (elitis.fr). 'Masai' **mirror**, from £312, Serena Confalonieri (serenaconfalonieri.com) ➤

From left 'Cala' **chair** by Doshi Levien, from £2,667, Kettal (kettal.com). 'Sumba' **fabric** (as curtain), £139.60 per metre, Sahco (sahco.com). 'San' **sofa** by Lionel Doyen for Manutti, £4,240, Go Modern (gomodern.co.uk). 'Geo' **pouf** by Paolo Grasselli, £624, Saba (sabaitalia.it). 'Ziqqurat' **storage cabinet** by Driade, from £7,380, Chaplins (chaplins.co.uk). 'Sequoia' **rug** by Élitis, no longer available. 'Tilda' **chair** by Francesco Bettoni for Baxter, £4,745, Silvera (silveraltd.co.uk). 'Majestic' **velvet**, £208.80 per metre, Pierre Frey (pierrefrey.com) **ED**

HOME OF THE
SIRENS' SONG
OF THE

This renovated Italian watchtower is a place steeped in myth, blessed with magical scenery

Words **AMY MOOREA WONG** *Photography* **MONICA SPEZIA/LIVING INSIDE**

Outdoor dining This shaded clifftop grove is the perfect location for dinner parties. Guests can even make use of the property's outdoor pizza oven **Exterior** Twenty metres high and with walls that reach up to three metres thick at the base, this watchtower is a true stronghold, built to withstand attack from pirates ➤

Perched on an outcrop of land on Italy's Punta Campanella, where the Sorrento Coast meets the cliffs of Amalfi, sits Norwegian architect Kristine Standnes's medieval watchtower. Surrounded by wild lemon, almond and olive trees, with views across the Mediterranean Sea towards the island of Capri, it's not hard to see why this area is a UNESCO World Heritage Site. Built in the sixteenth century as protection against attacking Saraceni pirates, and said to be the spot where the sirens sang to Ulysses in Homer's *Odyssey*, this place has magic in the air.

'When we took it over in the late 1980s, the tower was run down and almost in ruins,' says Kristine. 'My husband, Gianmattia, and I love restoration projects – this was such an unusual location and a rare opportunity, there are very few of these towers in existence.' The couple spent five years rebuilding, paying homage to the original construction materials. 'Most of the walls are original stone – we wanted to leave as much of it intact as possible, but also create a comfortable and contemporary feel.' The staircase, made using chestnut trees from the garden, is a new

addition; originally there was just a simple ladder, which would be raised when enemies invaded.

So, how to furnish such a landmark? 'There aren't many pieces of furniture that would suit this unique setting, but I do like to create a bit of a contrast by adding modern designs and artworks,' says Kristine. 'I want this to be a calming place to escape city stress and recharge.' Though regularly used as a stylish location for events and fashion shoots, the watchtower makes for an idyllic retreat for up to four people. Explore the picturesque landscape on foot, cook lunch in the garden's pizza oven, take a trip into the nearby villages or rent a traditional *gozzo* boat and explore the coastline. Alternatively, just sit on the sun terrace, relax and soak up the sea view.

HOW TO BOOK Naples airport is 65km away, Sorrento train station is 8km away. Airport transfers are available. From £526 per night for up to four people in two bedrooms. Holidays here are self-catered, although lunch and dinner can be provided if requested. Search for 'Sorrento Villa' at boutique-homes.com

'MOST OF THE WALLS ARE ORIGINAL
STONE – WE WANTED TO LEAVE AS
MUCH OF IT INTACT AS POSSIBLE, BUT
ALSO CREATE A CONTEMPORARY FEEL'

Exterior To bring more light into the watchtower, the homeowners added large arched windows into the historic stone walls. The white chair is a vintage '4860' by Joe Colombo for Kartell **Living room** The white sofa, a piece that has been in the family for a long time, is teamed with a 'PK61' coffee table by Poul Kjærholm for Fritz Hansen and a 'Tulip' side table by Eero Saarinen for Knoll. The oversized vintage 'Egg' lamp is by Max Ingrand for Fontana Arte and the antique kelim was bought in Istanbul **Stockist details on p167** ➤

'THERE AREN'T MANY PIECES OF
FURNITURE THAT WOULD SUIT THIS
UNIQUE SETTING, BUT I DO LIKE TO
ADD MODERN DESIGNS AND ART'

Opposite An olive green 'Platner' chair by Warren Platner for Knoll sits on top of hand-cut traditional Italian Cotto stone floor tiles bought in Naples **Above** A 1960s marble-topped 'Tulip' table and chairs, both by Eero Saarinen for Knoll, add some modernity beside the ancient stone walls **Stockist details on p167 ➤**

'MY HUSBAND AND I LOVE
RESTORATION PROJECTS – THIS
WAS SUCH AN UNUSUAL LOCATION
AND A RARE OPPORTUNITY'

Hallway A vintage 'Superleggera' chair by Gio Ponti for Cassina creates a reading nook beside the door made from local chestnut trees **Bedroom** Another 'Tulip' table for Knoll is placed next to the bed, which is dressed in softly crumpled local linens – for similar, try Society Limonta **Stockist details on p167 ➤**

THE SUN TERRACE IS THE BEST
PLACE TO ENJOY COOLING BREEZES
FROM THE MEDITERRANEAN SEA
AND GAZE OUT TOWARDS CAPRI

Bathroom An integrated granite stone basin is placed beside the large window, allowing breathtaking views.
The modern tap is from Boffi **Sun terrace** The white 'Voido' rocking chair by Ron Arad for Magis is the
perfect spot from which to watch the boats sailing to and from Capri **Stockist details on p167** ED

ANGLE POISE

The sharp angles and white interior of this New Zealand hideaway form a dramatic contrast with its wild surroundings

Words
AMY BRADFORD
Photography
**NATHALIE KRAG/
LIVING INSIDE**
Production/styling
TAMI CHRISTIANSEN

Living area A sofa from Trade Me, New Zealand's version of Ebay, is tucked into a sunny corner in front of the floor-to-ceiling window (try the 'Continuous' design by Faudet-Harrison, available at SCP). Soho Home sells similar cushions
Exterior Inspired by the structure of a tent, this home's pitched roof slopes downwards to create a discreet profile. The build was ecologically sound, as timber foundations were used instead of concrete, which could seep into the soil **Stockist details on p167 ➤**

f architect Chris Tate's holiday home on Waiheke Island, off the coast of Auckland in New Zealand, reminds you of a tent, there's a very good reason why. A few years ago, Chris took a camping holiday on a friend's country estate and it sparked the idea of building his own retreat from city life. 'I was lying in my tent, feeling very much at peace, when I realised that I could use its structure as a starting point for a small, low-maintenance home,' he recalls. 'While I was there, some kids let down part of the tent and that inspired the shape of the house I eventually built, with its uneven angles tapering towards the ground.' Inevitably, Chris decided to name his new home Tent House.

Five years in the making – it was completed in 2015 – the metal-roofed home is entirely bespoke. 'There were no pre-fabricated elements,' he explains. 'Because nothing was square, you couldn't give anyone accurate dimensions to work from. It was a question of being on site, using your eye and measuring everything out completely by hand.'

The interior is ultra-simple, with an open-plan living area, kitchen, office and guest room downstairs, as well as a bedroom and bathroom on a mezzanine level. The shape of the house allows for both sunnier spots and shadier areas – the former around the huge glass wall at the front, and the latter in what Chris refers to as a 'cool contemplation zone' at the back, sheltered beneath the roof canopy. The painted-steel spiral staircase creates a juxtaposition with the angular architecture, and the furnishings are almost completely white, in order to contrast cleanly with the forest landscape.

Although he rents out the house for holidays, Chris also comes here often with his wife Pony McTate, a crochet designer, and their sons Fergus, six, and Bambi, four. Sometimes, he visits alone to work when life on the family farm near Auckland gets too hectic. 'The house is comfortable all year round – Waiheke has its own microclimate, so it's never too hot or too cold,' he says. 'And the island is always a fun place to be, with its vineyards, beaches and bohemian village vibe. Even though we have neighbours, the greenery makes for a wonderfully private retreat.' *christatearchitecture.com*

HOW TO BOOK From Auckland International Airport, it's a 30-minute taxi ride followed by a 30-minute ferry journey to Tent House. Stays costs from £140 per night. Check availability and make bookings at tenthouse.co.nz

'THE HOUSE IS BATHED IN LIGHT AND CATCHES DAPPLED SUN ALL DAY. THE WHITE WALLS AND FLOOR REFLECT EVERY SUNBEAM'

Dining area The curves of the painted-steel spiral staircase are echoed in the white dining furniture: a 'Tulip' table by Eero Saarinen for Knoll and a set of 'Casalino' chairs, designed in the 1970s by Alexander Begge and still manufactured by Dutch company Casala. The 'Cactus' coat rack was designed by Guido Drocco and Franco Mello for Gufram in 1972. The floor is concrete, painted white to match the rest of the interior
Stockist details on p167 ➤

'THE HOUSE'S ANGLES CREATE A STEALTH-LIKE FORM IN THE FOREST AND A COMPLEX INTERPLAY OF LIGHT WITHIN'

Kitchen The ebony-stained MDF kitchen units are bespoke, complemented by a black sink (try John Lewis) and matching appliances, including a hob by Smeg. The 'Hee' bar stools are by Hay
Stockist details on p167 ➤

'I WAS LYING IN MY TENT, FEELING VERY MUCH AT PEACE, WHEN I REALISED THAT I COULD USE ITS STRUCTURE AS A STARTING POINT FOR A HOME'

Corridor This leads to the bathroom and laundry area. The chair is a 1960s piece by Australian brand Sebel – for similar in the UK, try The Peanut Vendor **Stockist details on p167** ED

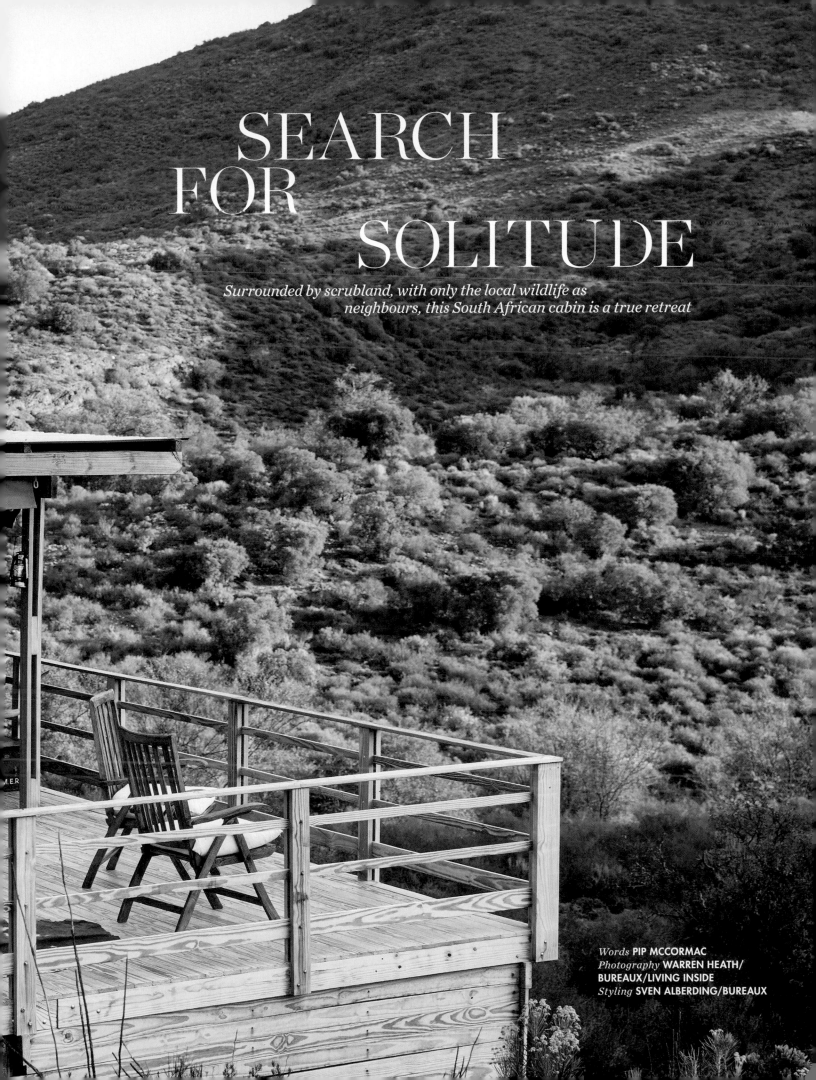

SEARCH FOR SOLITUDE

Surrounded by scrubland, with only the local wildlife as neighbours, this South African cabin is a true retreat

Words **PIP MCCORMAC**
Photography **WARREN HEATH/ BUREAUX/LIVING INSIDE**
Styling **SVEN ALBERDING/BUREAUX**

'It's very hard to put into words,' says William Mellor, struggling to do justice to the experience of relaxing on the terrace at Cabine du Cap in Little Karoo, South Africa. 'The valley surrounds you like a vast amphitheatre, and you feel completely removed from the world. Your senses are heightened, trying to pick out the different animal sounds.' It's easy to understand what he means. Rugged tufts of indigenous plants, an uninhabited landscape and a bleached-out quality to the light invoke a mood of cogitation at this off-grid ranch, just a two-hour drive from the Mellors' main home in the capital city of Cape Town.

'It all started with a dream to have an outdoor bathtub,' says William's wife Samantha, who now runs a collection of holiday homes with her husband. Indeed, the whole property was carefully planned around the placement of their custom-made galvanised steel bath: far enough away from the roof to enjoy an unobstructed eyeful of the star-washed sky at night. 'We sometimes put on the *Out of Africa* soundtrack, sit in the bath and watch the sun set,' she laughs.

The house is built on the site of what was once a ramshackle animal enclosure – but from very first sight, the couple could see its potential to be a place where they could escape the world. 'We fell in love with a material called Rhino Wood because of how it blends into the setting,' says Samantha. This sustainable, durable modified wood was used for the decking and expanding the living space. The large stone-walled fireplace was another new addition – 'essential for the cold winter nights,' notes William.

There is an air of carefree vacations to almost every aspect of life at Cabine du Cap, from lazy afternoons spent enjoying the outdoor living areas to the charms of the basic kitchen. 'When you go for walks, it's a lot like being in the south of France,' says Samantha, adding that the couple's four-year-old daughter Francesca is particularly fond of the opportunity for adventure afforded by the terrain. 'At night, the stars take you aback. I know, it sounds like a cliché,' William concedes with a smile, 'but you don't really understand until you're there: it's completely silent, the moon is like a spotlight... You stand there and all of your troubles disappear.'

Outdoor seating area Several of the chairs are from William's furniture brand Malawi Cane, while the white armchairs are an old set from his family, re-covered in linen **Stockist details on p167** ➤

HOW TO BOOK Little Karoo is a two- to three-hour drive from Cape Town. Prices start from £150 per night, including breakfast. The house has one double bedroom, with a luxury tent for an extra two people. To check availability and book, head to cabineducap.com

Outdoor terrace This area is used as a second living room, a place to shelter from the sun and take in the views. The seats and coffee table were made by an artisan in Cape Town **Kitchen** Small and rustic, this space has a farmhouse feel, which is complemented by the collection of copper kitchenware – try Rowen & Wren for similar utensils **Stockist details on p167** ➤

'You feel *completely removed* from the rest of the world. Your senses are *heightened*, trying to pick up the different *animal sounds*'

William and Samantha enjoy time spent lounging by the outdoor plunge pool with their daughter Francesca. But it is family dog Lacoste who is the biggest fan of the cabin's wild and remote surroundings ➤

Bedroom Now around 100 years old, this bed used to belong to William's grandmother. The wardrobe is from a vintage store in Cape Town. The basket is from Malawi Cane **Outdoor bathing** The shower enclosure is encased in Rhino Wood and stocked with products from Africology, while the tub is made of galvanised steel **Stockist details on p167** ED

ELLE
the Parisians' lifestyle

EYEWEAR

Discover the world of ELLE on elleboutique.com

ELLE
DECORATION
ESCAPE

ELLE DECORATION BEST OF BRITISH

From coastal design stores to city gardens, mind-expanding festivals and workshops to the ultimate spa break, make this the summer you explore the wealth of exciting things to do in the UK

LANDSCAPES
CHARLES JENCKS' GARDEN DESIGNS

American architectural critic, theorist and landscape designer Charles Jencks' cosmos-inspired gardens are jaw-dropping in scale and artistry. Take a trip to the privately-run sculpture garden **Jupiter Artland** near Edinburgh, which is open until 30 September – there, you can see Jencks' Cells of Life (above), a beautiful grassy exploration of the matter that forms every living being, with rolling hills and spiral ponds. Book a five-course dinner (available on 21 July; 18 August; 1, 21 September, £50) and delight in exclusive access at dusk (jupiterartland.org). Alternatively, head to **Northumberlandia**, Jencks' quarter-mile-long figure of a reclining woman, affectionately nicknamed The lady of the North, carved out of the earth, near the town of Cramlington (northumberlandia.com). ➤

SHOPPING
WHITSTABLE

For a hit of salty sea air, a taste of fresh Kent oysters and a peruse of interesting craft and design stores, head to Whitstable on the Kent coast. The picturesque seaside town is where artisanal joinery and design firm Kent & London began its business in a beach hut – it now has a showroom on London's Hackney Road, but the original store remains an ever-changing source of inspiration (kentandlondon.co.uk). Nearby, in a former fisherman's cottage, lies Frank, a gallery/shop purveying paper goods and contemporary homeware (frankworks.eu). Finally, pick up a woven basket or marble wall clock at The Union House boutique (theunionhouse.co.uk).

CULTURE TRIP
FESTIVAL NO.6, GWYNEDD

Welcome to Wales' take on the Italian Riviera: the technicolour village of Portmeirion (left) was dreamt up by wealthy traveller Sir Clough Williams as a reimagination of Portofino in the 1920s, and today plays host to Festival No.6, an annual music and culture weekender. If camping isn't for you, rent a local cottage or stay at one of the village's B&Bs after a day of listening to author Will Self give a reading on the piazza, partying to garage music in the woods and dining at a white-tablecloth banquet of locally caught fish by the sea's edge. From £180 for a weekend ticket, 6–9 September (festivalnumber6.com).

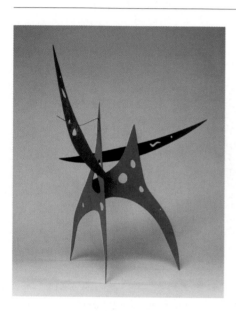

SCULPTURE
'ALEXANDER CALDER: FROM THE STONY RIVER TO THE SKY' AT HAUSER & WIRTH

Mobiles, sculptures (such as *Sword Plant*, left) and surrealist canvases will further brighten the bucolic landscape of Bruton, Somerset this summer, when this cutting-edge gallery's solo exhibition of the American 20th-century sculptor lands. Of particular note and charm are the handmade household devices (until 9 September; hauserwirthsomerset.com). For an after-show bite to eat, visit Roth Bar & Grill, the gallery's art-filled brasserie, or At The Chapel, a converted 17th-century church serving delicious Mediterranean fare (atthechapel.co.uk).

MOVIE MAGIC
FILMS BENEATH THE STARS WITH THE LUNA CINEMA

Known for cleverly pairing films (both classics and the year's big blockbuster hits) with fantastic pop-up outdoor venues across the UK, The Luna Cinema turns ten this year. To celebrate a decade of movie magic, it is putting on a stellar season. Highlights include *The Darkest Hour* beamed onto a screen in front of Blenheim Palace, where Churchill was born; *Jaws*, which can be watched from a dinghy on Brockwell Lido; and *Victoria & Abdul* at Queen Victoria's birthplace, Kensington Palace. New venues include Peckham Rye park and York Minster. Tickets from £13.50 (thelunacinema.com).

DESIGN FAIR
NEW DESIGNERS, LONDON

If you want to hunt for homeware that you won't have seen before, support the next generation of creatives or just pick up boundary-pushing and functional designs, visit New Designers in Islington, London. Britain's biggest undergraduate design extravaganza is an interiors industry favourite – it's where Thomas Heatherwick was talent-spotted in the 1990s. We're excited to see the One Year In showcase, revealing what 2017's graduates have been up to in the past year – particularly Joanna Hejmej's ceramic lights and Alexander Lohr's oak chair. 27 June–7 July, from £12.50 for a day ticket (newdesigners.com).

SPA
THE LAKE HOTEL

Achieve total relaxation at this new hotel and spa in The Lake District, the first outpost to be opened by new hotel brand Another Place, founded by the team behind Cornwall's Watergate Bay Hotel. Enjoy the scenery by kayaking across Ullswater, the area's second largest lake, or simply gaze at your surroundings from the ten-metre swimming pool, sauna and spa. After a long day's sightseeing or pampering, be sure to book a table at the hotel's Rampsbeck Restaurant – its pale green walls and crimson seats are stylish, while the cured Cumbrian ham and bitter leaf salad has to be tasted. From £200 per night (another.place/the-lake).

Beechleigh,
Hertfordshire

HOUSEHOLD GARDENS

The National Garden Scheme encourages green-fingered homeowners to open their well-tended lawns and flourishing flowerbeds to the public on one day a year, with the small admission fees (usually £5) going to nursing charities – more than £50 million has been donated to date. Pay a visit to one of our six favourites (ngs.org.uk)

TOWN PLACE GARDEN, SUSSEX
Look out for the box topiary in the shape of Henry Moore sculptures, grasses influenced by Dutch garden designer Piet Oudolf, plus 600 roses, dahlia-dotted potager and an 800-year-old oak tree for good measure. Open on various dates between 14 June and 8 July.

BAY TREE HOUSE, WINCHESTER
The rill and pleached (gardening-speak for trained to grow 'flat') lime tree square brings modern lines to this lush landscape of Mediterranean plants and blousy perennials, complete with a wildflower orchard. Open 5 July.

15 THE AVENUE, CHEAM, SURREY
Designed by Chelsea Flower Show Gold medallist Marcus Barnett, with box hedges pruned to resemble cloud formations, this garden also features a collection of contemporary sculptures. Open 28 May and 2 June.

THE JUNGLE GARDEN, LEEDS
'Gardening is an exercise in optimism,' reads the website for this takeover of a suburban backyard, overseen by homeowners Nick and Gill Wilson. The plot contains towering Gunnera plants, cherry-red orchids, a bamboo lodge and ponds filled with Japanese carp. Open 24 June and 29 July.

18 DORCHESTER GARDENS, LONDON
Open for the first time this year, this geometric garden, created by the house's owner, garden designer Sarah Oxby, is inspirational for its inner-city serenity. Olive and bay trees preside over voluminous blue-themed borders of lavender and hydrangea. Open 1 July.

BEECHLEIGH, HERTFORDSHIRE
On 25 August, you can visit this space by London landscaper Daniel Shea from 5–8pm. At this time of the evening, the fading light renders the golden grasses, dahlia beds, herb border of salvia, echinacea and lavender, and 13-metre reflective pool even more atmospheric. ➤

The Land
Gardeners

Firenza
Flowers

WORKSHOPS

*Experimental floristry is all
the rage. Learn how to make
breathtaking floral displays
at these inspirational courses*

THE LAND GARDENERS

Sign up to the 'Grow your own cut flowers'
one-day workshop held by The Land
Gardeners – the soil specialists, garden
designers and growers Bridget Elworthy
and Henrietta Courtauld – at either
their own plot in Oxfordshire, or
London's Flower Appreciation Society.
A ticket includes lunch, a handbook and
flowers to take home. 14 June and 10
October, £245 (thelandgardeners.com).

FIRENZA FLOWERS

For a masterclass on building almost
architectural floral displays, head to
Yorkshire, where arranger Fiona Pickles
of Firenza Flowers studio offers 'Large
scale installations' workshops. Fiona
provides ladders, barrels of blooms –
from dahlias to hedgerow berries and
crabapple branches – and expertise
on how to design and structure your
artworks. Lunch is included and pupils
are welcome to take the flora home with
them. £435 (firenzafloraldesign.co.uk).

Omar's Place,
Pimlico

FINE DINING

*No need to book a flight to
taste the world's most exciting
cuisines – simply book a table
at one of these London restaurants*

OMAR'S PLACE

Kudos to London design duo Sella
Concept, whose polished terracotta
walls, pistachio-coloured terrazzo and
end-grain wood flooring make arriving
at Omar's Place in Pimlico akin to
stepping into a sun-soaked tavern.
Egyptian chef Omar Shabaan has brought
the very best of eastern-Mediterranean
dishes from his homeland to this Grade
II-listed Victorian former pub – the
squid tartare and fresh lemons perched
on a slab of marble is as much a sculpture
as it is a starter (omarsplace.co.uk).

LAHPET

Over in Shoreditch, you'll find Burmese
kitchen Lahpet, which started as a stall
on nearby Maltby Street Market and
serves gloriously fragrant dishes, such
as *mohinga* (catfish and lemongrass
chowder) and tea leaf salad. Plus, the
interior's fantastic tiles are a real feast
for the eyes (lahpet.co.uk).

JIDORI

You can now find a pocket of Tokyo
in Covent Garden at Jidori, an ode to
yakitori chicken skewers and Japanese
style. Tiny izakaya bars inspired British
architect Giles Reid's design for the
space, which resulted in intimate rooms,
palest pink walls and bleached pine
furniture. Don't miss the ginger ice-
cream with miso caramel or the kitsch
karaoke room (jidori.co.uk). ➤

Jidori,
Covent Garden

Lahpet,
Shoreditch

Bishop's Palace, Wells, Somerset

HIDDEN SANCTUARIES

'Green Escapes: The Guide to Secret Urban Gardens' (£16.95, Phaidon) is an encyclopaedia of gardens that are open to the public, but not (yet) famous. Entries stretch from Kyoto to Tangiers to Antwerp, but it's the gates to grassy plots in the British isles that we plan to creak open this summer. Here are our four favourites

BARBICAN ESTATE'S BEECH GARDEN, LONDON

It's the contrast of concrete and rampant wildflowers that delights visitors to these gardens set among London's famous Brutalist buildings. Following a 2012 update, the book tells us that 'the monochrome geometry of the architecture is now softened and cheered by colourful, naturalistic plantings by Nigel Dunnett' (cityoflondon.gov.uk).

BISHOP'S PALACE, WELLS, SOMERSET

The Bishop of Bath and Wells' home, a palace built in 1206, has seven spectacular gardens through which we are all welcome to wander. The book describes the East Gardens as 'a plantsman's paradise, featuring a "hot border" with fiery flowers and exotic foliage'. This leads to the Wells Garden, where the city's natural springs fill shady pools surrounded by damp-loving irises and candelabra primulas (bishopspalace.org.uk).

THE HIDDEN GARDENS, GLASGOW

Scotland's first 'sanctuary garden' was funded by a non-profit organisation and purpose-built in 2003 as a peace-making plot of land in the city's multicultural Pollokshields neighbourhood. A rill now runs through borders of medicinal herbs, such as flowering comfrey and catmint, and the planting elsewhere echoes a mix of culture and religions, with bamboos, ginkgo, hazel and winter-flowering plum trees (thehiddengardens.org.uk).

ST DUNSTAN-IN-THE-EAST, LONDON

Built in 1100, the church that originally stood here was burned down by the Great Fire of London, then restored, only to be bombed in the Blitz. Its shell is now a public garden. We love how the Gothic architecture, including Christopher Wren's 17th-century steeple, is softened by roaming vines, trees and curving cobbled paths (cityoflondon.gov.uk).

SUPPER CLUB

WILD DINING IN THE FOREST, SCOTTISH BORDERS

Book now for an end-of-summer pop-up dinner in the forests of East Lothian, hosted by Amanda Farnese Heath, aka the Mad March Hare – a photographer and cook who grew up in an Italian household before moving to the North Berwick coast. The evening of 28 October will include an enlightening lecture on mushrooms by forager Monica Wilde (accompanied by a single-malt sharpener), then a trip to the magically decorated copse (right) for a candlelit seven-course dinner cooked over fire. Guests can stay in nearby treehouses. Dinner, £125; treehouse stays, £50 per person (themadmarchhare.com).

EXHIBITION

'ALL TOO HUMAN: BACON, FREUD AND A CENTURY OF PAINTING LIFE' AT TATE BRITAIN

'I want the paint to work as flesh does,' Lucien Freud said in 2009. In this blockbuster show of British portrait painters, it is startlingly clear that he – and his peers, who included Frank Auerbach and Paula Rego – achieved this demanding aim. Don't worry if you can't make it to London's Millbank before 27 August when the exhibition closes (tate.org.uk) – the show's curator, Elena Crippa, has written a book exploring how, where, when and why these artists painted the human form so engagingly (£25, Tate Publishing).

NEW ARTISTS

LIVERPOOL BIENNIAL OF CONTEMPORARY ART

2018 is the tenth year that this festival of contemporary art has been running, and it's as ground-breaking and exciting as ever. The theme for this year's ten weeks of artworks, special projects and programme of events is 'Beautiful World, Where Are You?', taken from the title of Friedrich Schiller's 1788 German poem questioning uncertainty on planet Earth. As you'd expect, there are provocative works on show across the whole city, including at venues such as the space-age Metropolitan Cathedral, the dockside Tate Liverpool and RIBA North. 14 July–28 October (biennial.com).

FESTIVAL

PORT ELIOT, CORNWALL

The eccentric Grade I-listed house and grounds of Port Eliot (right) have been hosting festivals since the punk and folk music 'Elephant fayre' of the 1980s, and this year, the event has changed again under new directorship. Alongside old favourites – swimming in the estuary and the literary pub quiz – will be Anna Jones cooking in the vast Georgian kitchen, comedian Robert Webb in conversation and fashion collector Daphne Guinness introducing visitors to the new Fashion Foundation in the walled garden, which will hold workshops, exhibitions and more. 26–29 July, day tickets from £62.50 (porteliotfestival.com).

PHOTOGRAPHY

'CATWALKING: FASHION THROUGH THE LENS OF CHRIS MOORE' AT THE BOWES MUSEUM

Known to some as the V&A of the north, County Durham's The Bowes Museum attracts stellar touring shows, but also curates brilliant new exhibitions in its own right. Check out its fantastic exploration of 'king of catwalk photography' Chris Moore's career highlights, starring snaps of all the 'supers' from Jerry Hall at YSL to Naomi Campbell at Vivienne Westwood (7 July–6 January 2019). The venue's public gallery also has a permanent collection, with works by Goya and Canaletto (thebowesmuseum.org.uk).

GARDEN FAIR

THE HAMPTON COURT PALACE FLOWER SHOW

For July's Hampton Court extravaganza, the RHS has commissioned four young, female garden designers to create four different outdoor spaces. The party-throwing garden by Anca Panait has been laid out to encourage conviviality and al fresco dining, and planted with herbs that echo the botanicals in gin. There is also a health and wellbeing garden by Alexandra Noble and Lilly Gomm's family garden, while London-based Lithuanian designer Ula Maria of Studio Unwired's focus in the 'Modern Antiquarian's Orchard' is contemporary design. Open 3–8 July (rhs.org.uk). ➤

Backwater eco-house, Norfolk

WEEKEND GETAWAYS

From a boathouse to a treetop dwelling, these refuges offer staycationers a breath of fresh air

BACKWATER, NORFOLK

Both Scandi and East Anglian boathouses influenced London studio Platform 5 Architects' design for this four-bedroom eco-house on the Norfolk Broads. The outside is clad in black-stained timber, while the interior is chic. There's also a lakeside terrace, jetty and rowboat. From £1,900 for a three-night stay in September (backwaternorfolk.co.uk).

CHURCH COTTAGE, COTSWOLDS

Make like William Morris, who summered at nearby Kelmscott Manor (now open to the public), and hole up at the beautiful Church Cottage in the same village. The stone five-bedroom farmhouse now has a light, bright kitchen that looks straight out through its patio doors to olive trees, potted lavender and a heated pool. From £551 for three nights (luxurycotswoldrentals.co.uk).

KUDHVA CABINS, CORNWALL

At Kudhva, sustainably-built lodges on stilts offer views down to the English Channel. Designed by New British Design studio's Ben Huggins, they have a rustic, pared-back kind of feel, with outdoor showers and no internet. Wake to the dawn chorus, cook breakfast over the fire pit and then go for a swim in the lake or surf in the sea before a soak in the hot tub. £114 per night (kudhva.com). ED

Kudhva cabins, Cornwall

Church Cottage, the Cotswolds

ELLE
DECORATION

INSPIRATION DIRECT TO YOUR INBOX

Sign up to our fortnightly email newsletter now to see even more of the stylish interiors, expert decorating tips, trend updates and essential buys that you love. Because sometimes a month is too long to wait for your next fix of ELLE Decoration

SIGN UP NOW AT

WWW.ELLEDECORATION.CO.UK/NEWSLETTER

STOCKISTS /

A
Africology (uk.africologyspa.com)
Agape (agapedesign.it)
Amazon (amazon.co.uk)
Amini Carpets (amini.it)
Andersen (andersen-ev.com)
Aram (aram.co.uk)
Artillerict (artilleriet.se)
Artisans of Devizes (artisansofdevizes.com)
Azucena (azucena.it)

B
B&B Italia (bebitalia.com)
Bang & Olufsen (bang-olufsen.com)
Bauwerk (bauwerkcolour.co.uk)
Baxter (baxter.it)
Benchmark (benchmarkfurniture.com)
Bert & May (bertandmay.com)
Billie Rose (billierose.be)
Boffi (boffi.com)
Botany (botanyshop.co.uk)
Brdr Krüger (brdr-kruger.com)
Brian Yates (brian-yates.co.uk)
Bungalow 8 (bungaloweight.com)

C
Casala (casala.com)
Cassina (cassina.com)
CC-Tapis (cc-tapis.com)
Chaplins (chaplins.co.uk)
Claybrook (claybrookstudio.co.uk)
Clé (cletile.com)
Clippings (clippings.com)

D
Dedar (dedar.com)
Dedon (dedon.de)
Designers Guild (designersguild.com)
Divertimenti (divertimenti.co.uk)
Dornbracht (dornbracht.com)

E
Ecora (ecora.co.uk)
Élitis (elitis.fr)
Empreintes (empreintes-paris.com)
Ex-t (ex-t.com)

F
Farrow & Ball (farrow-ball.com)
Fired Earth (firedearth.com)
Flos (flos.com)
FontanaArte (fontanaarte.com)
Fritz Hansen (fritzhansen.com)
Fromental (fromental.co.uk)

G
Gan Rugs (gan-rugs.com)
Go Modern (gomodern.co.uk)
Gufram (gufram.it)

H
Habibi (habibi-interiors.com)
Hansgrohe (hansgrohe.co.uk)
Hay (hay.dk)
Heal's (heals.com)
Horizn Studios (horizn-studios.co.uk)
Houseology (houseology.com)

I
Iittala and Arabia Design Centre (designcentrehelsinki.com)
Isle of Skye Paint Company (isleofskyepaintcompany.co.uk)

J
John Lewis (johnlewis.com)

K
Kettal (kettal.com)
Knoll (knoll-int.com)
Kollekted By (kollektedby.no)

L
La Doublej (ladoublej.com)
Liberty (libertylondon.com)
Little Greene (littlegreene.com)
Louis Poulsen (louispoulsen.com)

M
Magazyn (magazyn.be)
Magis (magisdesign.com)
Malawi Cane (canefurniturecapetown.co.za)
Mandarin Stone (mandarinstone.com)
Martinelli Luce (martinelliluce.it)
Maruni (maruni.com)
Mater (materdesign.com)
Minotti (minottilondon.com)
Molteni & C (molteni.it)
Moroso (moroso.it)

N
Nanimarquina (nanimarquina.com)
Napé (murano900.com)
Nicolette Brunklaus (nicolettebrunklaus.com)

O
Officine Saffi (officinesaffi.com)
Onora (onoracasa.com)
Osborne & Little (osborneandlittle.com)

P
Paint & Paper Library (paintandpaperlibrary.com)
Paola Lenti (paolalenti.it)
Pierre Frey (pierrefrey.com)
Piglet (pigletinbed.com)
Pinch (pinchdesign.com)
Poggenpohl (poggenpohl.com)
Poggi (poggidesign.com)
Roche Bobois (roche-bobois.com)
Rockett St George (rockettstgeorge.co.uk)
Roda (rodaonline.com)
Romo (romo.com)
Rowen & Wren (rowenandwren.co.uk)
Royal Botania (royalbotania.com)

S
Saba (sabaitalia.it)
Sahco (sahco.com)
Santa & Cole (santacole.com)
SCP (scp.co.uk)
Serena Confalonieri (serenaconfalonieri.com)
SG Gallery (sharongoldreich.com)
Silvera (silveraltd.co.uk)
Sirin (sirincopenhagen.com)
Smeg (smeguk.com)

Soane (soane.co.uk)
Society Limonta (societylimonta.com)
Soho Home (sohohome.com)
Sony (sony.co.uk)
Spartan (spartan-shop.com)
Stahl + Band (stahlandband.com)
Steamery (steamery.co.uk)
Stellar Works (stellarworks.com)

T
Tacchini Edizione (tacchini.it)
Terrazzo Tiles (terrazzo-tiles.co.uk)
The Conran Shop (conranshop.co.uk)
The Hub General Store (thehubgeneralstore.com.au)
The London Smiths (thelondonsmiths.com)
The Peanut Vendor (thepeanutvendor.co.uk)
Tom Dixon (tomdixon.net)
Tonic Design (tonicdesign.co.za)
Twentytwentyone (twentytwentyone.com)

V
Valspar (valsparpaint.co.uk)
Vio Gallery (viogallery.com)
Volga Linen (volgalinen.co.uk)

W
Wall & Decò (wallanddeco.com)
Wedgwood (wedgwood.co.uk)
Wittmann (wittmann.at)

Y
Yamakawa Rattan (yamakawa-rattan.com)

Z
Zinc Textile (zinctextile.com)
Zoffany (stylelibrary.com/zoffany)

STYLISH INTERIORS

Create your dream living space with our inspiring collection

BRITISH HANDCRAFTED SOFAS AND SOFA BEDS COMPLETELY CUSTOMISED BY YOU

Create furniture that suits you and your home with Willow & Hall's range of quality handmade sofas, sofa beds, beds and accessories.

Customising any item is easy. Simply choose from their range of 130 beautiful fabrics, pick the perfect seat cushion and, if ordering a sofa bed, select from three luxury mattresses. Everything is made to order by their skilled craftsmen in Britain who have over 35 year's experience. Delivery is free across the UK within four weeks plus they offer free no quibble returns. As a reader of Elle Decoration they're offering an exclusive 5% off all furniture until 27th June with code ELLE27618.

To explore their range visit their London showroom, shop online at **www.willowandhall.co.uk** or call 020 8939 3800.

Product featured: The Alderton Chaise Sofa or Sofa Bed from £1,720 or £1,870

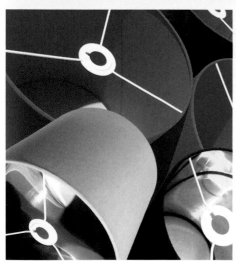

BYMARIE LONDON

Bespoke lampshade designer Marie offers an extensive collection of custom made lampshades, all made to order. Offering a mix and match range with over 22 fabric colours and 30 lining colours including metallics, they are perfect for someone looking for that extra-special something. Based in SW London.

For more details visit **www.bymarie.co.uk** or email: bymarie@me.com

BOBO1325

BOBO1325 is an innovative, socially conscious design house founded by Beth Travers.

Her unique designs have fuelled intrigue and interest from a wide range of clients who see their design choices as an extension of their identity.

BOBO1325's ability to create visually striking pieces, underpinned by messages such as climate control, gender equality and mental health have seen her reap praise from the industry. Distinctive, eye catching and not to be missed.

www.bobo1325.com

DAVID STUDWELL

David Studwell often uses figures that are synonymous with certain eras, in particular the swinging sixties and seventies.

Marilyn Monroe, Elizabeth Taylor and Steve McQueen all crop up in his prints, evoking a strong sense of nostalgia.

David recently collaborated with Sir Elton John and photographer Terry O'Neill to produce this six colour screen print with diamond dust. There is also a special edition available signed by Sir Elton John and Terry O'Neill priced at £4,000.

Title: 'Elton John: Home Run – Dodger Stadium 1975'. Screen print with diamond dust. Edition of 50. 95 x 63cm. £2,000.

www.davidstudwellgallery.co.uk
davidstudwell@gmail.com

DYEHOUSE

Yorkshire based furniture and homeware brand DYEHOUSE was founded in 2015 by award winning architect and interior designer, Mark Lee. Operating from a converted dyehouse, the brand draws inspiration from the natural, rural surroundings.

A meticulously conceived and crafted collection, created from materials that are largely characteristic of Yorkshire – principally oak, steel and leather.

All products are made to order and bespoke commissions are welcomed. You can see some of the range at the internationally renowned Yorkshire Sculpture Park.

Visit: **www.thedyehouse.com**
+44(0)1484 668 018.

AMMIL bench - blackened steel with leather wrap and solid oak shelf. Photo ©John Britton.

BLACKPOP
SHOW YOUR TRUE COLOURS

If you like your home full of character then Blackpop's lush wallpapers and fabrics set the scene with designs that punk up the rich tapestry of the past. "Mary", the award winning design featured, is one of three beautiful patterns created in collaboration with the National Portrait Gallery, inspired directly from their world renowned Tudor Portraits. These patterns are also available on cushions, scarves and silk note books. Proud to be made in the UK.

Email: info@blackpop.co.uk
www.blackpop.co.uk

HANDMADEINBRIGHTON.COM

The beautiful bespoke live-edge tables made by artisans Payne-Vigour come in all shapes and sizes, from huge slab walnut banqueting tables to small but beautifully formed statement piece oak kitchen tables such as this one commissioned by Dabrovska Design, London.

Every aspect of every piece is carefully considered, from the timber selection to the individually made legs, embedded items and occasionally a bit of technology!

hello@handmadeinbrighton
www.handmadeinbrighton.com

MISREMEMBERING
LANDSCAPES

Matt Jukes creates large-scale unique works on paper of forgotten places.
W: mattjukes.ink I: @mattjukes

INTERIORS & FLOORING

MASCULINE GLAMOUR

Interiors & Bespoke Furniture
casabotelho.com

CASA**BOTELHO**

T

WOODWORKS
BY TED TODD

The finest new, antique and reclaimed wood floors
www.woodworksbytedtodd.com

FIREPLACES, STOVES & HEATING

For stockists and to see the full range
of fireplaces and contemporary stoves please visit:

www.focus-fireplaces.com

Boafocus gas ©

focus®

design dominique imbert

**For 50 years,
Focus has been imagining
the future.**

JANEY BUTLER INTERIORS & LLAMA ARCHITECTS FORM PART OF THE LLAMA GROUP.
Creating award winning residential and commercial projects in the UK and abroad.

INTERNATIONAL AWARD WINNING ARCHITECTS & INTERIOR DESIGNERS.
The Coach House, Capesthorne Hall, nr Alderley Edge, Cheshire. SK11 9JY.

JANEY BUTLER
INTERIORS

W: LLAMAGROUP.CO.UK
T: 01625 861935
E: HELLO@JANEYBUTLER.CO.UK

RIBA

W: LLAMAGROUP.CO.UK
T: 01625 861936
E: INFO@LLAMAGROUP.CO.UK

Domestic & Contract Furniture
Designed & Manufactured in England

Tel: 0800 651 0001 | web: rigg.uk

rigg

ALISTAIR FLEMING

FINE ENGLISH CABINETRY

alistairflemingdesign.co.uk

DESIGNED & MADE IN LEWES, SUSSEX

The Headboard Workshop

www.theheadboardworkshop.co.uk
or call us on 01291 628216

Headboards & Beds | Ottomans & Stools | Sofa Beds & Chairs

barnby design

furniture design
handmade in HAY.

view the range at: www.barnbydesign.co.uk

Klarity

A selection of world class quality furniture luxuriously designed and manufactured using the finest materials.

tel: 0800 619 0599 | web: glassfurniture.co.uk

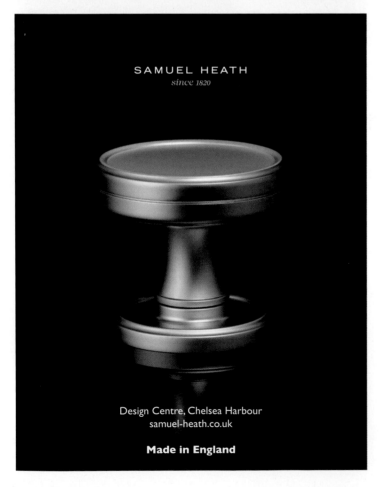

Make the perfect outdoor space...

Every item of furniture is made from durable, sustainable, grade-A teak, built to last and skilfully handcrafted for your ultimate comfort.

Versatile range of teak dining sets, garden benches, luxurious sun loungers and steamer chairs - perfect for contemporary or traditional settings.

Titan Teak Dining Sets*

CS395	4 Seat	£799.99
CS157	6 Seat	£1349.99
CS400	8 Seat	£1849.99

All tables are delivered with pre-drilled parasol holes and plugs.

40% OFF Matching Cushions
with Sets, Steamers, Loungers, Chairs & Benches

Teak Steamer Chair*
LT602 CA **£142.00**

Teak Sun Lounger*
LT176 CA **£163.00**

Bali Teak
Reclining Chair*
LT115 **£125.00**

Teak Planters from **£49.99**

Delivered assembled for your immediate enjoyment

For the most extensive range of quality teak garden furniture

Shop Now 24/7
cyan.co.uk

Call Mon - Sat 9am - 5pm
020 8655 6240

cyan

Visit Showroom
Unit 7 & 8 Gateway Business Park
Coulsdon London CR5 2NS

Sustainably Sourced
Grade A Teak Furniture

Indonesian **LEGAL** Wood

All items delivered fully assembled except Sun Lounger which requires minimal assembly. *Cushions and parasol sold separately. Prices valid until 31/07/18 and include VAT but exclude delivery.

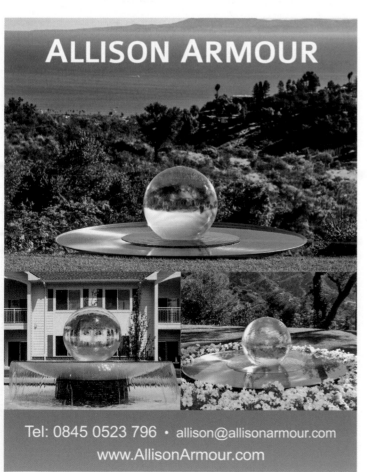

ALLISON ARMOUR

Tel: 0845 0523 796 • allison@allisonarmour.com
www.AllisonArmour.com

LIFE SIZE WILDLIFE SCULPTURE

Worldwide shipping

www.andrewkaysculpture.co.uk
(+44) 07740 306412

FINE PRINT /

'WIGWAM' LINEN BY ZINC TEXTILE

The new 'Geronimo' collection from Zinc Textile draws inspiration from the motifs of the native American Navajo tribe. This hand-sketched, striped 'Wigwam' print is especially vivid in the 'Klein' blue colourway.

'Wigwam' linen in 'Klein', £119 per metre, Zinc Textile (zinctextile.com)